The advanced Internet searcher's handbook

The advanced Internet searcher's handbook

Phil Bradley

LIBRARY ASSOCIATION PUBLISHING
LONDON

Published by
Library Association Publishing
7 Ridgmount Street
London WC1E 7AE

Library Association Publishing is wholly owned by The Library Association.

First published 1999

British Library Cataloguing in Publication Data

A catalogue record for this book is available from the British Library.

ISBN 1-85604-302-9

Typeset in Nissan, Franklin Gothic and Bergamo from author's disks by Library Association Publishing.
Printed and made in Great Britain by Bookcraft (Bath) Ltd, Midsomer Norton, Somerset.

Contents

List of figures

Preface

Welcome to the *Advanced Internet searcher's handbook*! Since I first became aware of the Internet several years ago I have been fascinated to watch the ways in which it has developed and grown. Since my first faltering footsteps onto it, I have been aware that it is an interesting but frustrating environment to work in. Despite all the hype about how easy it is to use, and how you can find almost anything you want to, I have found that unless you are a skilled searcher this is far from the case.

The aim of this book is to help you to search the Internet more effectively by giving you a better understanding of how search engines and related software and utilities work, allowing you to use them to improve your search techniques. I have also given lists of sites you can visit that will help further your understanding, and details of utilities that you can use to make life a little bit easier.

This handbook will be of use to anyone who uses the Internet to find information. It doesn't matter if you are taking your first steps into this new and exciting world or if you are an expert who uses it every day: you will find information, hints, tips, resources and utilities that will be of help. Although I have paid particular attention to the use that information professionals can make of the Internet, you should not feel excluded if you are from another profession – this book is designed to be of use to everyone who needs to find information quickly!

I have spent a lot of time exploring new and easier ways to obtain information more quickly and effectively by using search engines correctly, and by utilizing some of the many tools available. Here I have tried to explain some of these search engines and tools in detail, with the hope that you too will be able to search for the information you require in as painless a manner as possible.

I also have looked at intelligent agents, mailing lists, news-groups and so on, and have discussed how they work and why an information person would want to make use of them. I have also looked into my crystal ball to view some of the ways in which the Internet will be changing the life of the information professional into the next century.

Along the way I've discovered some interesting, sometimes amusing facts about the Internet which I've also shared with you – you will find them in the side panels. It has been an enjoyable trip along the 'information superhighway', and although I have not yet reached a final destination (indeed, I doubt that I ever will), I have witnessed many enjoyable sites (and sights!) and met many interesting people.

I ensured that the URLs listed in the *Handbook* were current before going to press, but the nature of the Internet is such that some may well have changed when you go to look at them at some point in the future. I hope, however, that your searching abilities will have increased enough to enable you to locate them for yourself!

You can read the *Handbook* from cover to cover, or you may prefer to 'dip in' and read chapters or sections that appeal to you, or that may help you answer a particular problem or question. At the end of each chapter I have given a list of URLs that I have referred to, and these have also been collated together at the end of the book as Appendix 3. These should prove to be a useful resource in their own right, and I have already referred to them quite a lot in my day-to-day work.

The Internet is changing all our lives, for better or worse, but mostly for the better, I feel. If you embrace the Internet, and learn to use it to its best advantage, I firmly believe that you will be all the richer for it. I hope that this book will prove to be of some help on your own personal journeys.

Acknowledgments

I should like to thank all the organizations and webmasters who gave me permission to use screenshots of their pages and utilities. All other screenshots are copyright of the original owners.

I would also like to thank all those people within the information industry who have pointed me on the right track, my clients who were understanding in any delays caused to their projects due to the time I spent writing, and to the people I have trained in the past for pointing out new places to visit and new software to explore.

I should also like to pay particular thanks to three people: Helen Carley at The Library Association for encouraging me to write this book and for her help and guidance during the process; Jenny Goodfellow for checking the typescript and making suggestions; and, finally, my wife Jill Bradley for her continued help and encouragement.

The advanced Internet searcher's handbook is dedicated, with all my love, to her.

1

An introduction to the Internet

Introduction

The Internet is not a new phenomenon, despite what you may read in the popular or the professional press. It already has a long and involved history; its creation and development profoundly affects the way in which it is used today and indeed how it will be used in the future. As each day passes, it is becoming clear that the Internet already affects or will affect almost every possible area of our lives. Pre-eminent among these changes are the ways in which information professionals view and use information. This chapter outlines some of the important developments of the Internet in order to provide background information. I do not intend to provide a history of the Internet, but if you are interested in this subject you are advised to visit **http://www.yahoo.com/ Computers_and_Internet/Internet/History/**, which provides a list of sites that cover this comprehensively.

An overview of the Internet

I can still remember the first time that I had an opportunity to 'surf the net'. As an aside, that is the first and last time you'll read that phrase, since it implies skimming over the top, desperately trying to keep your balance and ensure that you don't drown. The skilled user of the Internet knows what information is required and how to find it, retrieve it and go on to make good use of it. Perhaps a better description would be that of an underwater explorer (to adapt the surfing analogy) who is able to plot a course in the ocean to a specific point, plan and execute a dive, explore the wreck to obtain any treasure, and come back to the surface quickly and safely. This book will show you how to do just that.

When I first looked at the Internet I knew very little other

HINTS AND TIPS

I have included the addresses or URLs of as many sites as possible to allow you to undertake your own explorations, using the book as your starting-point. In some cases when referring to large subject areas I can only provide a brief overview and hope that you can use the site I refer to for more detail.

than what I'd been reading in the popular press. My friend Chris had just got an account with an internet service provider, and invited my wife and myself round for supper and surf. We planned to eat and then spend a couple of hours seeing what was out there. However, supper was not quite ready, so Chris and I began our first ever tour, while my wife read her book. We spent a long while trying to find something that was interesting (this was in the days before the arrival of helpful search engines); we downloaded a video of a NASA space launch, and generally had an enjoyable but frustrating time. We had become so engrossed that we failed to notice that we'd spent four hours in front of the computer, or that supper had burned to a crisp in the oven; my wife meanwhile was fast asleep on the sofa!

Frustrating though it had been, I became hooked on the Internet that evening, and looking back I can recognize that the problems we encountered were inherent in the system and exacerbated by our very limited knowledge. We didn't really know where we were going or how to find what we were looking for, and seemed to spend most of our time visiting one site which led us to a second, then to a third which sent us back to the first one again. It took a long time to download the information we wanted to see; the ten minutes it took us to retrieve that video was rewarded by about ten seconds of moving images! Of course, the Internet has come a long way since then, but users still find it a daunting and confusing place in which to work. For the new user it appears to be entirely chaotic, with neither rhyme nor reason behind it, but perseverance does pay dividends in a reasonably short space of time.

What the Internet is and what it isn't

■ It's not a single network
The Internet is a connection of networks throughout the world. Academic, military, governmental and commercial networks all combine to create the Internet. All the computers connected to the Internet make use of a common protocol, or way of passing data backwards and forwards, called **TCP/IP**. Data travels across ordinary telecommunications lines. As a

result it is very easy for individuals and organizations to connect to the Internet, thus increasing the amount of information available and also making it more difficult to find it! It also means that it is a robust system; when trying to obtain information from another machine somewhere else in the world, your software will work out the best routes to get from point A to point B, so even if some routes are unavailable you will still normally be able to retrieve the data that is required.

■ It's both local and global

The Internet isn't interested in geographical locations, and you can find the information that you need regardless of where you happen to be in the world. This is an important change for information professionals. When asked for information in a traditional library setting, an effective searcher will think geographically – is the information in a book on the shelf behind me? If not, is it available elsewhere in the library, or in a sister library down the road, or will it have to be retrieved via an interlibrary loan? All too often this geographical approach is at the expense of authority; while it might ideally make sense to talk to the San Francisco tourist board, for example, it is generally impractical because of the cost, the distance and the time difference. When using the Internet, contacting the appropriate source regardless of geographical location immediately becomes possible; it is simply necessary to find that source and your computer will immediately begin to retrieve data. If you as the information professional feel that the best way of answering a question is to refer the user to a local newspaper, for example, in many cases this is now possible. The Internet enables you to get the most appropriate information quickly, instead of relying on less precise information that may be easily at hand within the traditional library environment. Consequently, global information is available on a local desktop.

■ It isn't a single entity

The Internet isn't a single uniform resource. It is a collection of different resources, such as the World Wide Web, newsgroups, mailing lists, real-time 'chat' facilities, and much more. An effective searcher will be able to blend all of these

HINTS AND TIPS
I have tried to keep jargon terms to the minimum, but if you are puzzled by any of them and want more information you may like to visit a glossary of Internet terms at http://www.matisse.net/files/glossary.html

different resources into a single collection, using whichever elements are best to answer a query. A business librarian may prefer to use the Web to search financial databases and obtain company reports, while a public librarian may make considerable use of the ready-reference tools that are available, or post a difficult query to a newsgroup, hoping someone else may be able to come up with the answer.

■ It is possible to use a wide variety of hardware and software

There is no single standard software package used to access the Internet or any of its component parts. In a later chapter we'll look at some of the software which is available, some of which will be appropriate to some users and not others. Effective searchers will create their own library of software tools, specifically designed to provide assistance when seeking information. Similarly, there is no single type of computer which must be used with the Internet. It does of course help if you have a Pentium machine with a large hard disk, lots of memory, a sound card and printer attached, but it is not always necessary. Machines with a lower specification can also give good service without necessarily compromising data retrieval.

■ It is difficult to say who is in charge

The early networks which eventually combined to create the Internet were very often designed to be open systems that people or organizations could quickly and easily become a part of. Although some control was exerted (to limit participation to academic institutions, for example) no hard and fast rules were laid down. It is true that there are some organizations which are responsible for domain name registration, or for defining the way in which Web pages are written, but as far as the information professional is concerned there is no single authority which decides what information should be made available, or in what form. As a result, individuals and organizations are, by and large, free to do exactly what they wish. Consequently, information may be sparse in some subject areas, while there may very comprehensive coverage in others; information may be current to within a few moments or it may be years out of date; information may be authoritative or wildly inaccurate; much information will be of no use or may be offensive or illegal in some countries. You have to be able to assess value, currency and authority quickly and accurately without having necessarily knowing the publisher, the author, or the extent to which the information has been checked by peer review.

■ It's fast and effective

The Internet can be a very fast and effective way to communicate with other people or to retrieve information. A company report can be obtained in seconds, a bibliography can be compiled in minutes, and research which would otherwise take days may be completed in hours. As a result, it becomes possible to move from a 'just in case' paradigm in which it is necessary to have a store of information readily on hand in case it is required, to a 'just in time' model where information is not held locally but is retrieved as and when required to meet the needs of a specific enquiry. Effective information professionals can match their information needs to the availability of data on the Internet, and as a result may decide that there is no need to subscribe to a range of printed newspapers, for example, since many of them are readily available on the Web, together with archival information.

■ It is easy to talk to individuals or groups

Usenet newsgroups and mailing lists allow people with similar interests to keep in touch, to share knowledge, to express opinions or even just to gossip! Communities of interest are created which facilitate the free flow of information, freed from the confines of time or geographical location. This allows you to make contact with others around the world, to disseminate information to large numbers of people in ways previously not possible, and to draw on the experience of peers and experts in fields that you may never have known about before.

■ It's not all hard work

Information on the Internet covers almost literally every single subject that you could think of, plus a few more besides.

DID YOU KNOW?

Although no one organization 'controls' the Internet, the W3 Consortium is an international industry consortium which aims to develop common protocols to aid the growth and expansion of the Internet. They can be found at http://www.w3c.org

Professional information (however you care to define that) and personal or hobby information sit happily side by side, and it is as easy to discover the results of last night's lottery as it is to locate companies that sell chemical compounds. Even a small information centre is in a position to provide access to resources which previously would have fallen outside its remit. This does, however, bring with it the associated problem of ensuring that terminals are used to retrieve appropriate information, and not to download glamour pictures or worse!

■ It's not just for 'geeks'

Up until two or three years ago access to information on the Internet was by using a variety of tools that were less than user friendly. Veronica, Archie and Gopher services located and retrieved information, but these tools were difficult for end-users to master. Now, however, graphical interfaces, search engines and intelligent agents ensure that even novice users can quickly locate and retrieve information. This ease of use does come at a price: end-users will increasingly require training in how to critically assess the results they are achieving and the authority of the information they have obtained.

■ It's not well organized

Since no one 'owns' the Internet, everyone can do almost exactly as they please. No centralized authority means that people will publish the same information in different formats, incorrect or out of date information appears as well as accurate current information, and organizations and individuals will arrange their data and access to it in ways that please them. Flexibility on the part of the searcher is therefore paramount, coupled with the ability quickly to identify how information is arranged and to locate relevant data within a site.

■ It's growing at an enormous rate

There is little point in attempting to provide figures for the number of people who are connected to the Internet, simply because it is almost impossible to do, and even if it could be done, the figure would be very out of date by the time you read this. A generally agreed rule of thumb is that the Internet is doubling in size every year, in terms of users and Web pages. This means that information professionals have to work very hard to keep up to date with what is happening in this area. In order to be effective it is necessary to spend several hours a week locating new sites and trying new software. However, there are resources which can help in this process, and I have provided a list of some of them in Chapter 12.

If some of the terms used above make little sense at the moment, don't worry, because I'll be going into more detail on all these issues later on in the book. For now I'd like to provide you with further background on the different areas of the Internet I discuss in later chapters

Search engines

One of the characteristics of the Internet is the speed at which it has grown in the last two or three years. No one is quite sure of the size of the Internet or of the World Wide Web, and I've seen lots of conflicting statistics, most of which are quite out-of-date. However, a figure that I've heard often quoted is 200,000,000 Web pages, and I am happy to go along with that. Even if it is incorrect at the time of writing, by the time this book has been published and in your hands I would expect it to be accurate or even an underestimate.

In the early days of the Internet it was reasonably easy to find information or datafiles using a variety of software that was usually command driven: that is, you needed to type in the command you wanted executed, rather than using a graphical interface. However, with the proliferation of data brought about by the growth of the Web, these systems with such names as Archie, Gopher and Veronica became increasingly unable to cope. In order to overcome the lack of retrieval facilities, a number of organizations and individuals began to create their own software for searching and retrieving information. Unfortunately, very few of them had any kind of library or information background, so although they were (and are) doing a very sophisticated job of finding and

DID YOU KNOW?

If you want to find out how many people currently have access to the Internet you may wish to look at the Irresponsible Internet Statistics Generator at http://www.anamorph.com/docs/stats/stats.html

indexing all that information, the early implementations were quite crude. They were not designed for trained searchers, but for people who had never done a literature search in their lives, and as a result they did not make any use of Boolean operators, proximity searching, wildcards, truncation or any of the other things that we take for granted. Users simply entered any keywords that they felt were appropriate, and the search engines would retrieve hits based on their perceived relevance.

Over the course of time some of these search engines have hardly moved forward at all, and still the only way of finding appropriate Web pages is to throw as many search terms at them as possible and hope that you are lucky! However, some of the others have been through many new versions and are achieving the kind of sophistication that we take for granted when searching an online or CD–ROM-based database.

As information professionals the world over know, there is more than one way to catalogue or classify a book, and there is certainly more than one way to index the Internet! Chapter 2 explains in some detail how the different types of search engines work, and the advantages and disadvantages of using them. The next three chapters then look at particular search engines, how they can be used effectively and when they should be used.

Commercial databases

The history of commercial databases deserves a study in its own right, since the production of them, their use and subsequent developments closely match technological advances. However, this is not the place for such a discussion, so I will restrict my comments here to the way that the Internet has affected online commercial databases. As we will see later, database publishers are starting to make their databases available via the Internet. This is the case for traditional online publishers, and also increasingly for CD–ROM publishers. This means that the information professional has yet another avenue to explore when providing data access to the end-user.

This is a logical extension from the early provision of CD–

ROM databases in the information centre, since it is a way of moving data out of the libraries and onto people's desktops. Moreover, it is further influencing the job of the information professional, who is moving away from being the 'gate-keeper', or the person who goes away and obtains informa-tion for users, towards being the 'facilitator', who no longer performs the search, but establishes systems and trains users to obtain the required data for themselves.

The provision of commercial databases on the Internet is closely associated with electronic commerce. Once publish-ers can make their data available in this way, more flexible and varied pricing systems can be introduced. Users may, for example, buy a block of units that can be spent on retrieving any records from a publisher's collection of databases, or it may be preferable to continue to subscribe to a particular product. Publishers are going to have to work harder to keep market share, by providing value-added services, and we will explore some of the challenges facing the publishers, the information professionals and the end users in more detail in Chapter 6.

Virtual libraries and gateways

As we shall see, one of the problems of using search engines is that they return all the data they can retrieve indiscrimi-nately; the search engines are unable to make any qualitative judgements on the value or authority of the information they find. One of the advantages of the Internet is that it is very easy to publish information, and unfortunately that is one of its greatest disadvantages as well; no one owns the Internet, so no one is able to say 'this is good' or 'this is bad', and in any case, what is good to one person is bad to another. The whole question of authority is one which is mentioned to me at every training session I give, and so in Chapter 7 I have explained some ways in which the level of authority of a par-ticular document can be quickly assessed.

Information professionals have been taking an important role in this area, and over the last few years a large number of virtual libraries have been established. These attempt to gather together links to Web sites with authoritative, current, trustworthy and useful information. As a result, they are a very useful set of resources, which are all too often sadly ignored or badly publicized. The people who maintain virtual libraries have done a considerable amount of work for others in their subject areas, and these resources can provide a useful starting point for searches. Indeed, it may not be necessary to look anywhere else for the information which is required.

Virtual libraries are yet another example of the librarian acting as facilitator, and they can save searchers a lot of time by directing them to hard information. In Chapter 7 I explore the concepts behind them, and list some of those which are particularly useful, as well as explaining how they can best be utilized.

Intelligent agents

Search engines of all types, commercial databases, virtual libraries and gateways all have one thing in common: you have to visit them to find the information that is required. This is commonly referred to as 'pull technology'; the information has to be pulled down from a server somewhere. This may be perfectly acceptable for a lot of searches, but in situations where it is necessary to provide a current awareness service it very quickly becomes time consuming and laborious.

Intelligent agents help to overcome this problem by actively seeking out information that is needed, and they can be used to keep you up to date with what is happening in a particular subject area. Some of the most recent innovative agents can also be taught about the information that is particularly useful in any given situation, and are intelligent enough to go and explore the Internet on your behalf, sift what they find and present you with a small, focused and accurate collection of data.

There are many different types of intelligent agent, ranging from those which merely collate information in broad subject areas and make it available to you via a Web page (very often linked to specific search engines) to those that can be trained and which will then act independently on your behalf. Chapter 8 covers these agents in some detail, and explores the way in which they can be used to make searching an easier and more enjoyable experience.

Newsgroups and mailing lists

If the Internet is about anything, it is about people being able to talk to people. Much work is currently being undertaken in the fields of video conferencing and Internet telephony, for example, and though they have a long way to go before being fully functional, they are a good indication of the importance we all put on being able to talk to each other when and where we want.

Newsgroups and mailing lists are not as visually exciting or as 'sexy' as these recent innovations, but they have a long history, and are still perhaps the best way we have at present to talk to each other across the Internet. Unfortunately, they are also an under used resource, perhaps because they have been around since the early days of the Internet. In Chapter 9 I go into much more detail about what exactly newsgroups and mailing lists are, and explain how they can be of real assistance to the information professional. I give you some pointers on the different ways they can be used (both in technical and professional terms), and what software is required.

The information mix

As I have already said, the Internet is not one thing: it is a collection of different types of software and resources, used by many millions of people, all of whom have their own particular reasons to be using it. Never was this more true than when looking at how the information profession utilizes this collection of resources.

As a profession we are faced with an almost bewildering array of resources: traditional book based sources, online databases, CD-ROM (and shortly DVD technology), search engines, virtual libraries, newsgroups, mailing lists, intelligent agents – the list could go on and on. However, our key role has not changed; information has to be gathered, sifted, checked, and made available in one form or another for our users. The question of how this is done, though, is becoming more and more complex as each new facility is made available.

Once you have explored some of the sites I mention, and have installed and become familiar with the software needed, the next step is to try and make some sense of it all. As users also engage in the same process, and technology continues its rapid development, it this problem becomes more acute. It is necessary to try to blend and mix these resources together into a coherent package which is appropriate for your own user community. Where should the information be found? Should information be made available in a variety of formats? Is it possible to dispense with some traditional information resources and replace them with something else? How can users be encouraged to find information for themselves? What advances do we need to be at least aware of, if not actively planning to embrace them? I attempt to answer these questions in Chapter 10, and also point out where the Internet is perhaps leading us.

Better searching

A full understanding of the Internet and its resources is obviously invaluable, and a searcher cannot work effectively without this knowledge. I hope that this book will help you obtain this understanding, but a broad overview is only part of the picture. Sometimes it is necessary to explore some of the minutiae of systems and software. It is surprising just how much time can be saved daily by reducing each search by two minutes, or by using a shortcut here or there. In Chapter 11 I've collected together a number of hints and tips that should make searching and using the Internet a little bit easier and a little bit faster. I would estimate that you may be able to save several hours each week by incorporating them into your working methods.

Better software

The Internet, and particularly the World Wide Web, is constantly growing and increasingly in complexity as people explore new possibilities. In its early stages, the Web was text based, but it did not take long before still images, animated graphics, sound and multimedia were brought into play. Browsers are becoming equally sophisticated, with ever greater functionality.

Consequently, Web designers are always pushing the boundaries of what is possible, and commercial organizations, always seeking revenue, are providing ever more software to take advantage of the Web. In order to remain effective and to gain the most out of the system it is necessary to keep as up to date as possible, and the only way to do this is to install new software and to upgrade older versions.

In Chapter 12 I look at resources on the Internet that can help you in this area, and examine in more detail some packages which can make a very real difference to searching and using the Internet.

Where to go next?

The speed at which the Internet is growing means that it is not possible to stop still; if you try and do that you will find that you are out of date within a matter of days. The Internet is a little like a treadmill; once you have got on it and started to walk, it becomes difficult to get off it. Worse than that, the treadmill just goes faster and faster, and you have to run harder just to keep from falling behind. There are a number of Internet resources that are worth using to help keep you current, as well as organizations providing training courses. Chapter 12 also goes into detail on these resources, with the intention of ensuring that you don't fall behind – or if you do, that you are able to catch up again!

Summary

In this introductory chapter I have identified some of the key elements that affect the way in which the information professional is able to use the Internet, and have alerted you to the major areas that this book covers. I expect that you will find some chapters to be of more immediate interest than others, so feel free to explore those; each chapter stands on its own, and while they do make reference to each other, you can read them in any order that you wish.

URLs mentioned in this chapter

http://www.yahoo.com/Computers_and_Internet/
    Internet/History/
http://www.anamorph.com/docs/stats/stats.html
http://www.matisse.net/files/glossary.html
http://www.w3c.org/

Part 1

Mining the Internet for information

2

An introduction to search engines

Introduction

The Internet is often referred to (in my opinion incorrectly) as the 'Information Superhighway'.

The term gives the impression that it is fast and effective, getting you quickly from A to B in the twinkling of an eye. Furthermore, it implies that the ride is going to be a smooth one, with no bumps or potholes, and certainly no chance that you are going to break down.

Unfortunately, nothing could be further from the truth. In point of fact, I think a closer and rather more accurate analogy is that of the library I would expect to find in the type of gothic house you see in horror films: huge and rambling, with long corridors leading off into the middle of nowhere, small rooms packed with frequently used material in little order and yet other places shrouded in darkness from which one can hear rather nasty noises. The whole grand edifice is presided over by a half-insane librarian who is constantly coming up with new classification and cataloguing schemes. He implements them on a few hundred titles before thinking of a new idea, and begins again with a different scheme on some new materials which have just been dumped in no order on the floor. Meanwhile, minions of our insane librarian are busily working in different rooms, constantly arranging and rearranging their own collections, without reference to each other, and each convinced that they have the best collection and best scheme for its arrangement.

Unfair? Yes, perhaps it is, but only a little. We've already seen just how fast the World Wide Web is growing, and it is easy to let your eyes glaze over at the sheer amount of data that we're talking about. The Web *is* large and it *is* growing

DID YOU KNOW?
You can find the origins of this phrase, and many other quotes, by pointing your browser to http://www.quoteland.com/index.html

at a tremendous speed, and gathering speed under its own anarchic mass, but strangely enough it is, in the main, going in one direction. As a result, it is possible to impose some control over it and to put some structures in place. Chief among these are the different search engines, which prove to be of great assistance in allowing us to quickly find the exact piece of data that we require, sometimes in less time than it takes to articulate and type in the query.

I am not going to pretend that the search engines are perfect – very far from it! As we will discover, they all have their own shortcomings, and we are a long way from having a perfect interface or comprehensive index to the Internet. However, until we finally reach that holy grail we have to work with the tools that are available to us, and in this chapter I am going to give you an overview of the way in which the search engines actually do their jobs; the more you understand about search engines the easier they are to use and the more effective they become.

The rise of the search engine

I'll start by asking you a question: 'How many search engines do you think there are out there?'. The chances are that your immediate reaction would be to give me a figure in the region of perhaps a dozen or so. If you've just read the previous chapter, you'll already have learned not to underestimate the size of the Internet and the speed at which it grows, so you may be a little more confident in giving a larger figure, perhaps in the region of four or five hundred. You would still be a long way short of the mark, as there are over two thousand five hundred search engines that you can choose to assist you in finding the information that you require.

If you find this figure just too remarkable to believe, I'd ask you to hold back on your scepticism for a moment or two. While my question was not exactly a trick, I expect that you were thinking of one specific type of search engine, the type thta attempts to index the whole of the Internet, such as AltaVista or Yahoo!. If you'd said a dozen or so of that type you'd be a little nearer to a correct answer, though you'd still be out by rather a large number. When I posed the question I was thinking much more broadly than just that generic type of search engine – I was including lots of smaller engines which may only search one particular site, or one particular resource, such as a dictionary for example. Once you redefine search engines more broadly, the figure of two or three thousand becomes less implausible. If you are still looking at this page in disbelief, I'll point you towards a couple of search engines which list search engines as one of their functions – the Internet Sleuth at **http://www.isleuth.com** and Metaplus at **http://www.metaplus.com**, both of which I'll look at in more detail in Chapter 5.

Lets discuss this business of definition in a little more detail. There are basically four different types of search engine available to you:

- free text search engines
- index- or directory-based search engines
- multi- or meta-search engines (both terms are used interchangeably)
- resource- or site-specific search engines.

Free text search engines

Free text search engines are very easy to describe. You can simply search for any single word, a number of words or in some cases a phrase. You are not limited in any way as to your choice – you may wish to search for the name of a company, a line of poetry, a number, a person's name, a foreign language term, just about anything.

This approach has both advantages and disadvantages, as you would expect. Free text search engines are very useful if you know exactly what you are looking for, or if you are looking for a concept which can be defined in a small number of words. They are less useful if you want a broad overview of a subject, or are searching in an area that you don't know very well and consequently have no idea as to the best terms to use. There are a great many free text search engines available for you to use, and we'll look at some of them in later chapters, but for now if you want to break off reading and try one out I'd suggest that you go and have a look at AltaVista at **http://www.altavista.digital.com**.

Most of the free text search engines are unfortunately quite

DID YOU KNOW?

It is a common practice for organizations trying to sell pornography on the Internet to register site names which are similar to those of existing, reputable search engines, perhaps only differing by a single letter. Consequently you should take care when typing any Web address, and particularly those of search engines, in case you arrive at a site which contains information you'd really rather not see!

HINTS AND TIPS

If you search for two words, such as President Clinton, most free text search engines will translate that as a search for President OR Clinton, but will give a higher relevance ranking to those sites which contain both words.

primitive in their approach, and if you have used online or CD-ROM based resources you might be a little surprised. With a few notable exceptions, all that you can do is to type in a series of words. You cannot use Boolean operators, truncation or wildcard symbols, and you may not evenbe able to search for a phrase. Free text search engines are often aimed at the lowest common denominator, which is people who have never done any kind of searching before.

Relevance ranking

You may therefore wonder how you are able to retrieve any information of value from your searches, and the answer is that these engines use relevance ranking when they display results on the screen. They employ a series of complicated algorithms to order the hits into a list with the sites that they think you will be most interested in at the top, with the less appropriate sites lower down the list. Search engine designers all have their own ideas as to the most appropriate methods of ranking sites (which they change on a tiresomely regular basis), which means that you will get an entirely different set of records from different engines, even if you are using exactly the same search criteria.

I've listed some of the criteria that are used by free text search engines below, but please note that not all search engines will use all of these criteria, and even if they do they may well give different weighting to them.

- word/term/phrase appears within the meta tag element
- word/term/phrase appears in the title of the Web page
- word/term/phrase can be found in a main heading or subheading of a page
- the number of times the word/term/phrase appears in the body of the text.

HINTS AND TIPS

The meta tag element is a hidden element on a page which is seen by the search engine, but not the viewer. It is a way in which the author of the page can define key terms and concepts contained within it. Search engines often use the meta data to calculate the page's ranking in the returned results.

Index- or directory-based search engines

These search engines take a rather different approach to providing you with information on the sites that you might want to visit. Their emphasis is on classifying information under a series of major subject headings, and then subdividing these into a tree structure of more specific headings, and sites are listed as appropriate in this directory structure. If this approach sounds familiar, that is because it is, as anyone who has ever used a library classification scheme will know.

The advantages of this approach are obvious. The subject headings and subheadings can be used to guide the users through the vast mass of information until they are able to locate exactly the right section which covers the area that they are interested in. An in-depth knowledge of the subject is not required, since the users can stop drilling down through the tree at any point, check one or two sites to see that they are in the right area, and then continue to focus and re-focus until they get to a reasonably small number of sites which can then be viewed individually if needed. Probably the most famous of these index search engines is Yahoo!, and you may wish to break off from reading to go and have a look at it – Yahoo! is to be found at **http://www.yahoo.com**.

You will not be surprised to know however that there are also disadvantages inherent in this approach, and these lie in the initial construction of the headings structure, which may well show up individual biases. For example, if you are look-ing at Yahoo!, one of the main subject headings together with its subheadings is:

Government
    Military
    Politics
    Law
    Taxes

My American readers are probably looking at this and scratching their heads, wondering what is wrong with it. This is perfectly understandable, because from an American point of view there is nothing wrong with it. However, a British reader might look slightly askance at the subheadings, since we would expect to find some of them elsewhere in the hierarchy. Yahoo! has attempted to overcome this particular problem by providing country specific versions of the index, as we shall discover later. The basic point still stands, how-ever; when you use an index search engine you are at the mercy of the people who put the structure into place. If you assume that a subject is going to be found under one series of subheadings, you may spend a lot of time drilling down into one section of the index, when what you want is to be found elsewhere. To use the example above, a logical assumption might be to look for information on the last British General Election somewhere in that Government/Politics hierarchy, but in actual fact information on this subject is found under Regional/Countries/United Kingdom.

Many of the organizations which have produced index based search engines have recognized that this may be a problem for their users, and have created a free text search box which can be used to quickly identify exactly where within a hierarchy the users will find information about their subject of interest. We'll see how some of the major engines have done this in Chapter 4.

Multi- or meta-search engines

The next type of search engine isn't really a search engine at all, since a multi-search engine doesn't actually search anything itself. Instead it takes your query and passes it onto a selected group of search engines. Once the results start coming in from these individual search engines, a multi-search engine displays the results on the screen. The more advanced engines will collate the results, removing duplicates, and put them into some sort of sensible order.

Multi-search engines are useful if you want to try and obtain a comprehensive listing of Web sites that cover a particular subject. Individual search engines may well not be fully comprehensive, and one may index sites that another has missed and vice versa. Searching each of them individually is going to take time: you must locate the URL, visit the engine, input your search, wait for the results and then visit the pages you find useful before repeating the whole process somewhere else. Using a multi-search engine means that you only have to visit one page, and all the results are brought back to your screen, therefore limiting the amount of work that you have to do.

Unfortunately, this strength is also a major weakness of a multi-search engine. Since you are submitting your search to a number of different search engines, they all have to be able to understand the syntax that you are using. Therefore either you have to know that each of the engines understands the symbols used to run a phrase search, for example (which means more work for you), or you are limited to just putting in various keywords without being able to focus your search more tightly. Some of the more sophisticated multi-search engines are now able to translate your query into the correct syntax for each search engine, but this cannot be guaranteed, so you should check, rather than automatically rely on this happening.

There is a second type of multi-search engine, which is perhaps even less like a search engine than the type that I have described above. These enginges simply provide you with links through to lots of other search engines, without even giving you the opportunity to input search terms to be forwarded to them. If I were being pedantic I would refer to sites such as this as 'launchpad' sites, rather than search sites in their own right. They can be very useful, however, by providing you with links to search engines and other resources which you might otherwise have never found at all – or, if my experience is anything to go by, which you would have found the day after you really needed them!

If you are keen to try out a multi-search engine, you could visit the Internet Sleuth, **http://www.isleuth.com** or if you want to have a look at the second type of engine, pay a visit to MetaPlus at **http://www.metaplus.com**.

Resource- or site-specific search engines
The final category of search engines is perhaps the largest, but paradoxically the least well used, probably as a result of their diversity. A resource-specific engine may well have been created simply to search one particular resource, such as the Bible, a dictionary or an encyclopaedia. There is very lit-tle which can be said generally about these engines, since they are all very different to look at and to use. One point which it is important to make, however, is that generally the resources which they index are not indexed by other, more general search engines, and the reasons for this will become clear in the next section of this chapter. Since these resources are site specific it is not possible to point to a complete listing

of them, but the Internet Sleuth does provide you with access to a number of them.

One type of resource-specific search engine which is worth mentioning here in a little detail is what is generally referred to as a 'people finder' or 'people searcher'. These engines will, as the name implies, find people on the Internet for you, a little like directory enquiries. You obviously need to know a little bit about the person you're looking for, such as their name, or part of their name (this isn't as silly as it sounds, since you can find references on the Internet to me as Phil Bradley, Philip Bradley or philb), where they come from (either their geographical location or where they post messages from), and any other information you have available. A people searcher will then attempt to locate individuals in its database that match the information you have provided, and will list them for you, thus allowing you to contact them. Usually the e-mail address is given, but in some cases you can also discover their geographical address and even phone number.

How search engines work

In order to use these resources effectively, it is necessary to have some background knowledge of how they work. Most of them make use of 'spider' or 'robot' utilities which spend their time crawling the Web looking for new sites, or sites which have changed since the spider last visited. When they find new or updated pages, they copy this information back home to be included in an updated version of the index at the search engine site. The spider will also follow any new links which it finds and repeat the process until it cannot find any more new pages, at which point it will retrace its steps and follow a new route.

This has a number of implications as far as the searcher is concerned. Given the size of the World Wide Web, this is a full-time job, and even the fastest computers have trouble keeping up with the flood of new pages onto the Web. This has been overcome to a certain extent in that Web site authors can contact search engines to inform them of new or updated pages which should be included in the indexes. As a general rule, priority is given to checking these pages, and in some cases they can be checked and added to a search engine index within a matter of seconds. However, if the author does not do this, it may take several weeks or even months for the pages to be located and indexed.

Search engine database currency

Consequently, when a search is run using a search engine, the results will only be a snapshot of the Web as it existed at some time in the past. That might be a matter of moments, or it may be days in some cases. Depending on the subject you are looking for, this may be a major problem or a minor inconvenience, but it should always be kept in mind. It may be necessary in some cases to completely change your overall search strategy; if you are looking for information on the latest earthquake, or the death of a celebrity, you will probably get the information you need by checking a newspaper Web site which is updated hourly, rather than by relying on some of the more general search engines that I have discussed. To be fair to them, however, within hours they were indexing and returning Web site addresses which related to the death of Diana, Princess of Wales.

Unfortunately, while search engines may be slow to provide searchers with new sites, they also will retain information on Web pages that no longer exist. It is quite common for an author to delete a page from a Web site when it is no longer required, and the only way that the search engines can discover this is to try to re-visit the page in order to re-index it. When an engine cannot find the page after a number of attempts, it will assume that the page no longer exists, and it will be deleted from the engine's index of sites. However, since there may well be a gap of weeks or even months between the author deleting the page and the engine discovering this, it will continue to include the page in the lists of results which are returned from a search. Do not be surprised, therefore, if you attempt to visit a page, only to be given an error message that states that the page cannot be found. Make a note of the page and try again later, but if it fails every time the page in question has probably been deleted by the author or moved to another location.

Not all search engines work on the principle of spiders,

DID YOU KNOW?
Nineteen new Web pages are published every four second.

and a good example of one which does not is Yahoo!. This search engine requires Web page authors to visit their site and register their pages into the most appropriate category (or categories) that Yahoo! covers. (If this isn't clear, don't worry – either visit Yahoo! yourself, or skip to Chapter 4 now to get some more information on Yahoo!.) Therefore, you are to some extent at the mercy of the authors, because if they index their pages incorrectly or obscurely this will lessen your chance of finding them when doing a search.

Meta-search engines do not index pages themselves in either of the ways described above. As mentioned earlier, they simply connect to search engines and run searches. The results obtained therefore rely on the ability of the engines used to provide current and comprehensive results.

Who owns the search engines?

Search engines are created by anyone who has the time, money and skill to devote to creating one. The Internet has few rules and regulations, so anyone can (to a greater or lesser extent) do exactly what they want to, and some organizations and individuals have decided that, for a variety of reasons, they wish to establish and maintain search engines for people to use. Most engines will provide you with some sort of background as to their origins in case you are interested in such things, but in most cases they were created because someone wanted to; it really is as simple as that. Some organizations could see there were commercial possibilities to be made out of having a Web site that gets visited thousands, if not millions of times a day, and I would hazard a guess that far more people now know about the Digital Equipment Corporation as a result of their creation of AltaVista than through seeing advertisements about them in the press.

How much do they cost to use?

Search engines take a considerable amount of time to establish and maintain. This requires full-time staff, expensive computer equipment, advertising and communications. It may therefore come as something of a surprise to discover that there are very few engines that charge end-users to search them. You are free to connect to your search engine of choice, interrogate the database and move on to view sites that interest you. In the training sessions that I run, people often express amazement that all of this information is given away freely, so if you are also surprised by this, do not worry – you are not alone!

Advertising

The answer to the question is, however, very simple, and can be summed up in a single phrase – 'advertising revenue'. Despite what I have just said about organizations giving away information and use of their facilities, the Internet is commercially driven, and this is best demonstrated by looking at the number of advertisements on Web sites offering a whole host of products. Almost all search engines include banner advertisements from other organizations enticing viewers to visit the sponsoring site; and once you visit, you will be faced with some very skilful attempts to part you from your money. Advertisers work on the theory of maximum exposure for maximum profits, and nowhere is this more evident than on a search-engine page. If an advertiser has a product for sale which costs £/$100 and places an advertisement for it on a site which is visited 10,000,000 times a day (which is not uncommon), if only 1% of people who see the banner visit the advertiser's site, and only 1% of them buy the product, that means a revenue stream of £/$100,000 per day! Consequently, they will be prepared to pay a reasonably large sum to the owner of a site that commands that many visitors.

Advertising placement

The subject of Internet commerce is much too large for the scope of this book, so I will not say very much more about it, other than to point out that it is possible for the astute searcher sometimes to make use of the advertisements. Placement of advertisements is becoming more sophisticated now, and if you run a search on some search engines for keywords such as 'gardens, gardening, flowers' it is likely that the banner advertisement which gets displayed on the results screen will be for a site thta sells gardening equipment, or it may be for an Internet florist, for example. Consequently, if you want to find such organizations, it could be quite useful to spend a few moments browsing the linking site.

To generate the maximum advertising revenue, it is in the best interests of the owners of search engines to encourage as many visitors as possible, which means having increasingly powerful search software, easy and advanced interfaces, and so on. Indeed, many of the larger search engines are now offering free e-mail addresses for life, Web space, personalized news services, and anything else they can think of to encourage visitors to return time and time again. Therefore, although in one sense searching is entirely free, in another sense you do actually pay by having to download an advertisement every time you view a page of results.

Summary

In this chapter I have outlined the major types of search engine and how they can be used. In order to search the Internet successfully it is necessary to match the search you wish to do against the type of engine and your level of knowledge of the subject. Each search engine will provide different results, based on the data contained in their indexes and the way in which they rank results for relevance.

None of the search engines is perfect, and all have their own particular advantages and disadvantages. The successful searcher will have a good understanding of the rationale behind their design and working methods. In later chapters I look at the different types of engine in more detail, and focus on a number of particularly important and popular ones.

URLs mentioned in this chapter

http://www.quoteland.com/index.html
http://www.isleuth.com
http://www.metaplus.com
http://www.altavista.digital.com
http://www.yahoo.com
http://www.metaplus.com
http://www.searchenginewatch.com
http://www.amazon.com

3

Free text search engines

Introduction

In this chapter I look in more detail at free text search engines; how they can assist the searcher, search methodologies and so on. I focus on one free text search engine in particular, AltaVista, but also point you towards others which work in a similar fashion, namely Lycos, HotBot, and Euroferret.

Free text search engines:

- will accept any term the user wishes to search for
- can search for terms in any combination
- can search for phrases as well as single words
- allow users considerable flexibility in choosing how to search.

AltaVista

AltaVista is one of the best known and oldest search engines available on the Internet (the other being Yahoo!) and was launched on 15 December 1995 at **http://www.altavista. digital.com**. On its first day it received 300,000 visits; it is now 'hit' over 20,000,000 times per day. The AltaVista Search Public Service was the brainchild of researchers at Digital Equipment Corporation's Palo Alto Laboratory, and research into the project to index the World Wide Web began in the spring of 1995. Work began in earnest during the summer of that year, and the whole project was up and running within 6 months.

The aim of the AltaVista service is to index the entire World Wide Web, and the AltaVista team has estimated that they have indexed over 100,000,000 Web pages, making it

DID YOU KNOW?
AltaVista was the code name of the project and was not adopted as the name of the service until two days before it was launched.

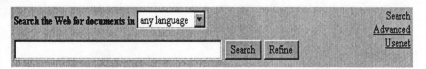

Fig. 3.1 *AltaVista search box*

the largest of the search engines. In theory, therefore, the majority of Web pages are stored by Digital on their servers, making it a good backup system, but I'm not sure that this would be a good thing to rely on!

HINTS AND TIPS

The Boolean operators are AND, OR, NOT, although some search engines require users to write AND NOT rather than NOT. They are the basis on which any search for two or more terms is run. 'Cat AND dog' will give a set of results which contain both terms; 'cat OR dog' will give a larger set in which the results have only to contain one of the two words; 'cat AND NOT dog' will limit the results to records that only contain the word 'cat', but not the word 'dog'.

Searching AltaVista: easy search

When AltaVista is displayed on your screen the most important element is the search box as shown in Figure 3.1.

To begin with, we'll ignore everything other than the white rectangle, which is the place in which you type your query. Since AltaVista is a free text search engine, you can type in anything you wish, and it will attempt to find Web pages which match your search criteria. Please keep in mind that AltaVista will automatically OR searches together unless you tell it otherwise. This inevitably leads to large results, but don't let this put you off. AltaVista will rank the Web pages it retrieves for relevance according to its own algorithms, by displaying what it thinks are the best possible matches first, with the less relevant ones further down the page.

Narrowing a search using truncation

As a result, a search using only one or two terms is not going to work very well, since the searcher is not giving the search engine very much to go on. A better search strategy would therefore be to include as many different terms as possible, since one of the ways in which AltaVista works is to give the highest relevance score to Web pages which include all of your terms, or failing that, which include the greatest number of them. Consequently, if you were doing a search for '*Jaguar cars*' it would make sense to do a search for '*Jaguar car cars automobile automobiles vehicle vehicles*' and so on. Alternatively, I could have saved myself a few keystrokes by using the asterisk '*', forcing the search engine to look for any words that start with the letters chosen, and any others which appear after the '*'. If I had truncated my search term at *car*★ AltaVista would have found matches for: *car*, *cars*, *cart*, *career*, and so on. However, in this case I would have retrieved far too many records which had nothing at all to do with cars, so while I would have saved a few moments typing I would have wasted more time in the long run having to skip over records that had no relevance to my search.

Weighting search terms

AltaVista does give your first term greater weight than the other terms. However, that would not stop it from finding a site which contained all the terms requested with the exception of *Jaguar* and deciding that such a site was more appropriate than a site which just contained the key word you really wanted to find. We therefore need some way of telling AltaVista that some terms are more important than others, and to do this we use the plus (+) symbol. This tells AltaVista that it must find sites which contain that particular word, with the other chosen terms being of less importance. Our search strategy would now look like this: '+*Jaguar car cars automobile automobiles vehicle vehicles*'. It will come as no surprise that we can also use the minus (-) symbol to exclude words which we are not interested in. Looking through the results which are returned from the above search I would not be surprised to find sites which use the term jaguar as the large wild animal, so I could include -*cat* -*animal* in the search strategy as well. Our search, which has now expanded to: '+*Jaguar car cars automobile automobiles vehicle vehicles* -*cat* -*animal*' is getting rather long and cumbersome.

Phrase searching

We do have another option available to use, which is to look for a phrase. AltaVista makes use of double quote marks (" ") to indicate that we wish to search for a particular phrase. As a result I may find that my search yields better results if I do a search for '"*Jaguar cars*"', which is shorter and neater, leading to a smaller and more appropriate set of results. I can now ignore the possibility of retrieving Web pages which refer to the wild animal, since it is unlikely that pages would refer to both the car and the animal, or if they do it will only be a very small number. You'll also note that I'm using a capital J

HINTS AND TIPS
Most search engines are now using the plus and minus symbols instead of making the users type AND or AND NOT, but you should still check with individual search engines, since this is a convention, not a rule.

HINTS AND TIPS

Not all search engines allow you to run a phrase search, so check on their help screens, but if they do, you will almost always get a smaller, more focused set of results.

HINTS AND TIPS

Remember to turn this option off when you start a new search, or you will be excluding or requiring search terms that related to the previous search you did, giving very odd results! AltaVista does not do this automatically for you.

in my search, and there is a very good reason for this. If you use a lower-case character AltaVista will automatically look for and retrieve both lower- and upper-case versions, but if you use upper-case AltaVista restricts itself to finding exact matches. This is very useful if you are searching for someone whose name is Brown, for example, in that you can, generally speaking, limit your search to surnames rather than for brown-coloured things. (It does not exclude the possibility of finding the word 'Brown' at the start of a sentence referring to coloured objects, but we can't have everything!)

Refining searches

Although I have been able to limit my search to a smaller number of results, I will still be retrieving a set which is much bigger than I want to have to work my way through. However, AltaVista has also considered that, and if you look back at Figure 3.1 again you will notice that there is an option to refine the search. This can be very useful in cases when you are running a search which is quite broad, or when you are not certain of the best terms to use. The 'refine' feature may well also suggest other terms which you had not considered, so it can act as a useful 'prompt' in the same way that some natural-language mapping or 'suggest' features work in interfaces provided by CD–ROM publishers.

Figure 3.2 shows you what happens when you choose the 'refine' option. AltaVista displays a list of terms which it thinks might be appropriate to the search which you have run. You can then choose to require, exclude or ignore '...' the terms by using the pull down menu options. Re-running the search will automatically add in the '+' or '-' symbols for you.

If your browser is a recent version it should be able to view pages which use Java applets. Java is a programming language that allows Web designers to create more interactive Web pages. It has only fairly recently been introduced, so if you are using an older browser you may find that pages containing Java applets do not display correctly. If your browser understands Java, you can choose to view a graphical representation of the terms and their relationships to each other by choosing the 'graph' option which is to be found in the top

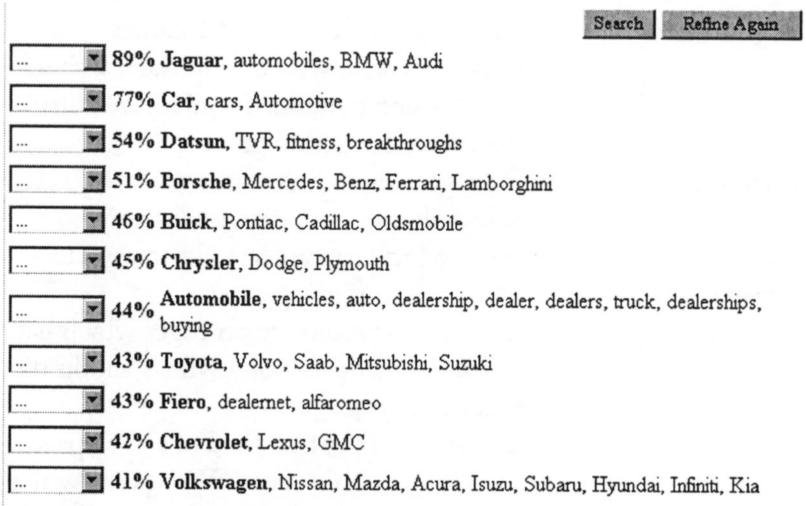

Search   Refine Again

... 89% **Jaguar**, automobiles, BMW, Audi

... 77% **Car**, cars, Automotive

... 54% **Datsun**, TVR, fitness, breakthroughs

... 51% **Porsche**, Mercedes, Benz, Ferrari, Lamborghini

... 46% **Buick**, Pontiac, Cadillac, Oldsmobile

... 45% **Chrysler**, Dodge, Plymouth

... 44% **Automobile**, vehicles, auto, dealership, dealer, dealers, truck, dealerships, buying

... 43% **Toyota**, Volvo, Saab, Mitsubishi, Suzuki

... 43% **Fiero**, dealernet, alfaromeo

... 42% **Chevrolet**, Lexus, GMC

... 41% **Volkswagen**, Nissan, Mazda, Acura, Isuzu, Subaru, Hyundai, Infiniti, Kia

Fig. 3.2   *Refining a search using the AltaVista Refine feature*

right–hand corner of the 'refine' screen. This option works in a very similar fashion to the main refine option as shown.

Refining searches using switches

AltaVista has a number of switches which can be used in combination with single terms or phrase searches to sharpen the search and to narrow it down further. These all take the format <option>:<search string>, and a list of them is included below, with examples:

anchor:text	for hypertext links
	anchor:titanic would find Web pages which use the word 'titanic' as a hypertext link
applet:class	for finding pages which use certain named Java applets
	applet:fred would find any Web pages which used an applet of class fred
domain:domainname	such as uk, de, jp and so on
	domain:uk would limit results to just those pages with .uk in the domain part of the address
host:name	for pages hosted at a site with a particular host name
	host:philb would return sites such as **www.philb.com**

image:filename	for images with specific filenames *image:clinton.gif* would limit the search to pages which contained a gif image with the filename clinton.gif
link:URLtext	for pages which link to the named URL *link:philb.com* would give a list of Web pages which contained links to my site
text:text	for words in the page text *text:widgets* would return pages which had the word 'widgets' somewhere within the text of the page
title:text	for words in the title field of a Web page *title:library* would return Web pages which had the word 'library' in the title
url:text	for pages with certain words or phrases in the URL *url:microsoft* would give find Web pages that contained the word 'microsoft' somewhere within the URL

Of these perhaps the most useful are those to limit your search to specific countries (a full list of the two-letter abbreviations for countries is included in Appendix 2) or within the URL of the Web page. By limiting your search by country you will exclude references to the rest of the world. This is an option which should be used with care, of course – there is no reason why someone in the USA should not publish a page about the English Civil War, for example, and by limiting your search to just UK pages you may be missing out on some potentially valuable information.

However, if your initial search does produce too many possible matches for you, it can be a productive approach, particularly if you are looking for pages which refer to a particular place or region. There are many locations called 'Essex', for example, and even limiting that to 'Essex County' does not stop references coming up to Essex County in the USA, or alternatively to the County of Essex in the UK if you're particularly interested in just those in the USA. A search strategy which looks like '+*"Essex County"* +*domain:uk*' will overcome that problem. (If you're interested in Essex County in the USA simply replace the '+' in front of domain:uk with a '–' to exclude British references.)

This search strategy does, however, have some other limits, particularly if you are looking for commercial companies. Many UK-based companies use the convention of having a URL in the form **http://www.mycompany.co.uk**, but this is just a convention; it is not a requirement. My own URL is **http://www.philb.com**, for example, which gives you no indication at all as to where I am based, or indeed what the subject content of my Web site happens to be. Consequently, if you use the domain switch to reduce the number of pages you retrieve, be aware that you may be excluding valuable information.

The option of choosing to search in the URL may be worth considering, since it will simply return a list of pages which include the word or phrase you have asked for within their URL. A search for *url:library* would return pages such as: **http://www.philb.com/library.htm** and **http://www. libraryland.org**. However, it would not give you pages which included the word 'libraries' in the URL or the word 'library' in the main body of the text. Nonetheless, it is reasonably safe to assume that a good Web page designer is going to create pages named in such a way as to reflect their content.

DID YOU KNOW?
My site is actually based in Manchester UK, just in case you were wondering!

Focusing a search

Let's start to put some of these things into practice and see how we can reduce the number of hits which AltaVista offers us. The following searches were run in January 1998, so you'll get different results if you run the searches yourself, but they should illustrate the point.

'Jaguar car cars automobile automobiles vehicle vehicles' produced a total of 494,138 hits.
'Jaguar car cars automobile automobiles vehicle vehicles –animal –cat' reduced this to a total of 26,036
"Jaguar cars" as a phrase search gives us 1,548 references
'+"Jaguar cars" +domain:uk' further reduced this to 293 hits.
'+url:Jaguar +domain:uk' gave the very reasonable number of 8 hits.

jaguar car cars automobiles
Click above for the RealName (sm), the easy web address for company and
product names.

1. Grand Touring Automobiles 1996 Jaguar XJ-R
[URL: www.webpeddler.com/dealers/autos/grandto...ouringcar17.htm]
A Special Collection Of the Finest Previously Owned Jaguar, Lotus, Aston
Martin, Rolls Royce & Bentley Automobiles On The Net
Last modified 10-Mar-98 - page size 5K - in English [Translate]

2. Grand Touring Automobiles 1995 Jaguar XJS
[URL: www.webpeddler.com/dealers/autos/grandto...ouringcar27.htm]
A Special Collection Of the Finest Previously Owned Jaguar, Lotus, Aston
Martin, Rolls Royce & Bentley Automobiles On The Net
Last modified 10-Mar-98 - page size 5K - in English [Translate]

Fig. 3.3   *Partial results from an AltaVista search*

You will of course get different results with different combinations of the syntax, but the examples above should give
you some ideas of how to proceed with your own searches.

Viewing results

Once you have run your search, AltaVista will display the
results on the screen for you to look at. I've reproduced a
sample screen in Figure 3.3.

The first line gives you the title of the page (as defined by
the Web-page author), followed by its URL. Then you see a
brief summary of the page, which is taken either from the
first few words that AltaVista finds, or from a special 'meta'
tag used when designing pages. Beneath that you see the 'last
modified' date and the size of the page. There is also an
option to translate this information into another language,
which is discussed in more detail in a moment.

If you wish to go directly to one of the Web pages, you can
click on the title element, and your Web browser will cut the
link with AltaVista and take you to the selected site.
However, there is a small icon to the left of the full URL of
the page, and if you click on that, the browser will open a
new window for you, while keeping your existing AltaVista
search screen open for further reference. This can be particularly useful if you want to view several sites in one go, or if
you would prefer not to keep clicking on the back/forward
buttons of your browser to move between pages or sites.

The example in Figure 3.3 has just two results, but in most cases you will find a number of hits displayed on the screen for you, with more available on subsequent pages. The first ten references are displayed on the screen, and you can move to the next page by simply clicking 'next' on the button bar at the bottom of the page, or by choosing a specific page of results to view. In most cases, there will be little point in going beyond the first couple of pages of results; either because you have found the information that you need, or because your search was not as focused as it might have been; if you're still turning up appropriate pages after you've looked at 20 or 30 sites, you should re-run the search, making it tighter.

Searching AltaVista: advanced search

If you take another look at Figure 3.1 you will see that there is an option in the top right hand corner for an Advanced Search. Even if you are an experienced searcher, I would suggest that you spend some time with the easy search screen to begin with, just to get a feel for the way the search engine works. When you decide to move on to the advanced features, you will see a screen which looks something like Figure 3.4.

As you can see, the search element of the screen does not appear substantially different from the easy search version, with the exception of a Boolean expression input field and a pair of date boxes. You should consider using the advanced search screen once you have become familiar with the general search process, or when you have a very specific query in mind. Most searches can be run perfectly well using the sim-

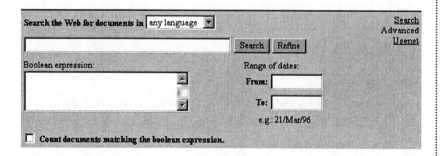

Fig. 3.4 *AltaVista advanced search screen*

ple form, but the major disadvantage of it is of course that AltaVista controls the relevance-ranking process. In the advanced format you have more control over how words or phrases are ranked, Boolean operators can be used to greater effect, and you have control over the date field.

Another difference will become apparent as soon as you attempt to run a search, which is that the '+' and '–' switches do not work – you must use Boolean operators, and they should be in upper case. AltaVista gives you an alternative here, however, and allows you to use the characters & for AND, | for OR, ! for NOT, and ~ for NEAR.

The date range allows you to just retrieve pages which were updated during a particular period of time, using the dd/mmm/yy format. This can be very useful if you wish to run a search on a regular basis to retrieve just those documents added or modified since the last time you ran the search. (If you do not enter a date, AltaVista defaults to the current year, which means that you may get a rather odd result if you are searching on 2 January!)

The ranking box (the unlabelled single-line input field) is also very important – if you do not use it, AltaVista will not rank the results which it retrieves for you, and you will be likely to end up with an unusable set of results. You can either re-enter some of the terms that you have already entered in the Boolean expression box, or you can add more terms which further define your search. To continue with the automobile example from earlier in this chapter, we might decide to run a search for '*Jaguar AND cars*' and rank the results using the terms '*renovation*' and '*restoration*'.

The advanced search facilities also allow you to make use of parentheses ( ) in a manner similar to that which you might have experienced if you have used any online or CD-ROM based search engines. The AltaVista help pages give a nice example here which is worth repeating: '*president AND ((George NEAR Bush) AND ((Bill OR William) NEAR Clinton))*'.

You will also notice from the previous example that AltaVista allows you to make use of the NEAR operator, and there are times when this will be more effective than doing a phrase search. For example, if you wanted to do a search for cattle breeding and did a phrase search for '*cattle breeding*', that is exactly what you would get. You would therefore potentially miss any references to 'breeding cattle' or 'cattle; problems associated with breeding'. The NEAR operator overcomes this problem, since it will find Web pages on which the two terms appear, in either order, within ten words of each other, so in this case a better search would be '*cattle NEAR breeding*'. Unfortunately it is not possible (at the time of writing) to define the number of words between the two keywords that counts as 'NEAR' – AltaVista predefines this as up to ten words.

A final useful switch which AltaVista has available is the wildcard function. This allows you to broaden out your search to include plurals, or anything which starts with a given sequence of characters. For example, if you want to start by doing a broad search for anything to do with libraries, you could try '*librar**', which will retrieve a set of records including library, libraries, librarianship, librarian and so on. The disadvantage of this approach is that you may retrieve a huge number of hits, so you should use it with caution, or right at the end of the word, just to catch a plural ending.

Searching AltaVista: Other facilities

We have so far covered both basic and advanced search features, concentrating on the advantages and disadvantages of the available syntax. However, AltaVista also allows you rather more flexibility than that, and if you once more refer to Figure 3.1 you'll begin to see an indication of some of the other options that are available. One of these is to change the default option to search the Web. If you choose the Usenet option in the top right-hand corner you are given an opportunity of searching Usenet newsgroups. I'll leave this for the time being, since I talk about newsgroups in Chapter 9.

Another is the option of choosing to search in a particular language. This feature was introduced into AltaVista in July 1997. It allows you to limit a search to just a single language, which at first sight doesn't appear to be particularly valuable. After all, if you include a foreign-language word you would expect that the vast majority of pages which you turn up are going to be in that particular language. However, if your first language is something other than English the value of the option becomes much clearer, since using it will eliminate any English pages, allowing you to work with a smaller, more focused set of results. AltaVista is able to do this because it employs dictionary based algorithms to work out the language of the page, as a result, pages which are written predominately in English, but which include one or two foreign words, are correctly classified as English.

If you do find a foreign-language page which looks interesting, but you are unable to understand the language in question, all is not lost, since the AltaVista introduced another new feature at the end of 1997, allowing you to translate pages into and from a variety of different languages. I've used this a few times, and while the translation is not perfect (and does sometimes include some of the howlers that computer-generated translations create!) it is usually enough to get by with.

I'd next like to draw your attention to the other options available on the right hand side of the search box, which I've reproduced in Figure 3.5.

AltaVista seems to have been re-inventing itself recently in

Fig. 3.5   *Other AltaVista search options*

recognition of the fact that a free text approach is not always the best way to run a search. (If you recall, we discussed this problem in Chapter 2.) Let's start by looking at the 'Browse Categories' option. If you click on this option you are taken to a new page, part of which I've reproduced in Figure 3.6.

The way this works is rather obvious: all you have to do is to choose a search subject, type it into the Search box and click on Go! Alternatively, you can click on a specific subject area. The page then refreshes to give you a second level of options, then a third and son on. Figure 3.6 illustrates this option at a point where I have chosen my major heading and then several subheadings.

I chose the option of 'Computers & Internet', then 'Business on the Net', then 'Intranets'. Once you begin to drill down into the categories, the arrow indicates that there are further categories to explore, or the small page icon indicates that a new page of sites will be displayed.

Returning to the options in Figure 3.5, AltaVista also gives you an opportunity to search for specific individuals, or for businesses. Unfortunately, these are not as helpful as they might first appear since they are geographically limited to the USA. Both of the search screens allow you to fill out information such as name or business type and location, and then they provide you with a list which matches the criteria. So essentially what we have here is a White and Yellow pages

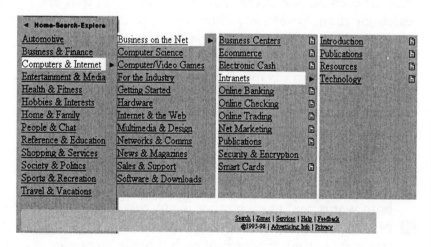

Fig. 3.6   *AltaVista browse by category options*

guide to the USA, which is obviously quite useful if you just need US-specific information, but has little if any value if your search is global, or for another country. I would suggest in those situations that you make use of different search engines, and in Chapter 5 I have provided a list of ones that I think are worth looking at. AltaVista does have servers based in other locations around the world, but at the time of writing they only offer a basic service, without the tabulated options discussed above. However, this might change in the future, so it is worth keeping a weather eye open.

Lycos

Established in May 1994, Lycos at **http://www.lycos.com** is one of the oldest of the search engines, and began as a project at the Carnegie Mellon University. Lycos used to be just a straightforward free text search engine, allowing you to input any terms you they wished in order to locate appropriate Web sites, but in common with other free text search engines it now also provides a directory listing of sites in a 'Web Guide' hierarchy. The Web guides are further divided into sections on 'community guides', 'mini guides', 'top ten listings', and some have ready-canned searches on popular issues of the day.

Figure 3.7 shows the opening Lycos search screen, which easily and quickly allows you to type in the words or phrases you want to find, and either to run the search there and then, or click on one of the radio buttons to get Lycos to search for all the words, any of the words or the exact phrase. The first drop-down box also allows you to search the Web, UK and Ireland sites, books, sounds or pictures.

Lycos also has an advanced power search feature. Using this you can incorporate Boolean operators directly into your searches, and the search engine also has powerful facilities for adjacency searching. Features offered include the following operators:

- ADJ – club ADJ football retrieves sites which contain both words next to each other in any order.
- NEAR – football NEAR club retrieves sites where both terms are within 25 words of each other in any order.

DID YOU KNOW?

Lycos comes from the Latin for 'wolf spider'

HINTS AND TIPS

Always check to see if a search engine offers help screens - not all do, but they can be very useful and provide valuable tips on search techniques.

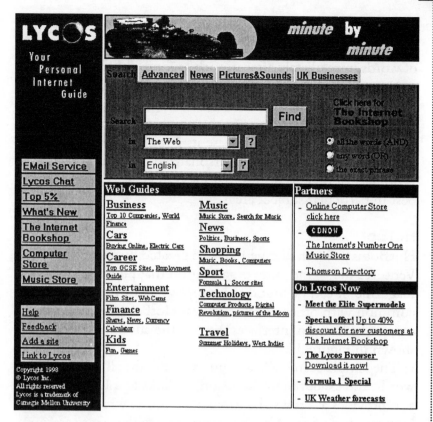

Fig. 3.7   *The Lycos simple search screen*

■ FAR – club FAR football retrieves sites which contain both words more than 25 words apart.

■ BEFORE – football BEFORE club is the same as the AND operator, but the first word must come before the second word, any distance apart.

It is also possible to specify the order of words by including O (for order) immediately before the operator:

■ OADJ – football OADJ club is equivalent to searching for "football club"

■ ONEAR – football ONEAR club retrieves sites where the terms are within 25 words of each other and football comes first

■ OFAR – is like ONEAR except that the terms must be more than 25 apart.

If the default of 25 words separating terms is not appropriate, this can be changed by adding a forward slash and the number of words immediately after it, such as football NEAR/5 club.

Naturally, these operators can all be combined, leading to very powerful search structures.

In common with other search engines, Lycos is adding new features in order to increase its popularity; it offers e-mail services, chat rooms, a personalized news service and a 'Top 5%' of reviewed sites that Lycos reviewers feel are the best in particular subject areas.

HotBot

HotBot is a search engine that was created by Wired Ventures Inc. – the same organization that publishes *Wired* magazine; it can be found at **http://www.hotbot.com**. In common with other search engines, HotBot provides both easy and advanced interfaces; part of the advanced interface is shown in Figure 3.8

The simple search allows you to search for all words, any words, the exact phrase, a person, or links to a URL. HotBot also provides a 'browse by category' option, which has the look and feel of the AltaVista approach, with major categories such as 'Computers and the Internet', 'Business and Finance', 'Travel and Vacation' and so on. Once you click on one of these categories, they are then subdivided into more specific sections, and so on. HotBot has links to search for other types of information, such as Usenet, Yellow and White Pages (US only), e-mail addresses, domain names, classified adverts, top news sites, homes and loans, stocks and shareware.

The Supersearch facility (the HotBot name for their advanced interface) is very flexible, with considerable functionality. Searchers can use all of the options previously described, and also limit the search by date, domain or location (including continents, rather than just by individual countries). One particularly nice feature is to limit searches to pages which include certain types of media, such as sound files or video. This is very useful if you need to look for information in a variety of formats – you could, for example, search for sites referring to the moon landings, and by limit-

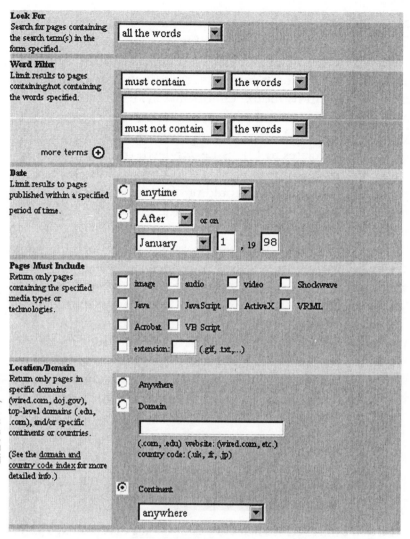

Fig. 3.8   *HotBot advanced search features*

ing this to sound and video sites you could retrieve pages that include transmissions of conversations between NASA and the astronauts as well as video footage of them engaged in moonwalks.

One final worthwhile feature of HotBot is that there is a series of links into articles from *Wired* magazine relating to issues of the day. These may prove to be a useful overview of a particular subject, such as Internet censorship for example.

Euroferret

Euroferret at **http://www.euroferret.com** is slightly different from the previous examples of free text search engines, in that it takes as its focus European sites, including over 25 million pages in its index. Unfortunately, it specifically excludes **.com** sites, which means that a site such as mine will not be indexed, even though much of what is available on my pages relates to UK issues. Indeed, this is particularly ironic in that Euroferret itself is at a **.com** address, which presumably means that it could not include any of its own pages in its index! A screen shot of the Euroferret search page is shown in Figure 3.9.

Euroferret takes a much simpler approach to searching than the search engines previously discussed in this chapter, even going so far as to list as an advantage that it does not use 'arcane boolean terms'. However, it does have two interesting approaches to locating information. Once you have run your search (and you do at least have the option of instructing the engine to match any/most/all words) you are presented with a screen which suggests stemmed words that can be included in a refined search. It also allows you to mark

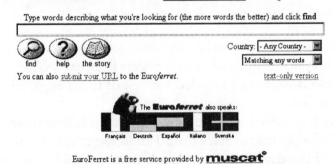

Fig. 3.9 *Euroferret search page*

Web pages that appear to be relevant to the search being conducted. Euroferret can then use the data from those pages to construct a refined search, which will hopefully result in a much closer set of hits.

A final advantage of this particular engine is that it is possible to restrict results to Web pages from any specific European country.

Other free text search engines

There is almost no limit to the number of free text search engines that are available, and it would be quite possible to write an entire book on them, rather than just a single chapter. If you do not feel inspired to use any of those which I have already listed, you may wish to explore some others for yourself, and I have listed some URLs below to get you started. It should not be regarded as a complete list, however.

AOL NetFind:	**http://www.aol.com/netfind/**
C|Net Search:	**http://www.search.com**
EuroSeek:	**http://www.euroseek.com**
Excite:	**http://www.excite.com/**
GoTo:	**http://www.goto.com**
InfoSeek:	**http://www.infoseek.com**
Look Smart:	**http://www.looksmart.com**
Northern Light:	**http://www.northernlight.com**
SearchEurope:	**http://www.searcheurope.com**
SurfStorm:	**http://www.surfstorm.com**
Webcrawler:	**http://www.webcrawler.com**

Summary

In this chapter I have gone into detail on how to use free text search engines, using AltaVista as my major example. Almost all free text search engines are now offering some sort of directory approach as well, but their major strength lies in their ability to translate free text terms into a meaningful search, and to return a list of results based on a relevance ranked approach.

Some of them are more sophisticated than others, and the advanced search facilities are constantly improving. Given this rate of improvement, it should not take very much longer before they offer the type of search techniques which online and CD-ROM systems have been offering for many years.

URLs mentioned in this chapter

http://www.altavista.digital.com.
http://www.lycos.com
http://www.hotbot.com
http://www.euroferret.com
http://www.aol.com/netfind/
http://www.search.com
http://www.excite.com/
http://www.goto.com
http://www.euroseek.com
http://www.infoseek.com
http://www.looksmart.com
http://www.northernlight.com
http://www.searcheurope.com
http://www.surfstorm.com
http://www.webcrawler.com

4

Index-based search engines

Introduction

Free text search engines are just one way of finding the information that you need on the Internet. They are very good if you know exactly what you are looking for and can identify it using a small number of keywords or phrases. However, they are less useful if you require a broad overview of a subject, or if you are unfamiliar with a subject and its technical jargon. This is where index-based search engines are much more appropriate.

Index-based search engines:

- arrange data in a structured fashion
- make use of headings and subheadings going from the general to the specific
- usually rely on Web authors to submit pages to the engine
- depend on their category structure for their success
- are generally quite simple to use, and appeal to novice searchers
- are useful if you want a broad approach to a subject
- are useful if you are unsure of what keywords to use in a search.

Yahoo!

The first index-based search engine which I'll look at in detail is Yahoo!, which was started in 1994 by two students at Stanford University, David Filo and Jerry Yang. It can be found at **http://www.yahoo.com**. It started when the two decided that they needed some sensible way of keeping track of their interests on the Web, rather than continuing to use their own large and cumbersome lists of Web sites. They developed software to allow them to quickly locate, identify and edit materials, and over the course of time Yahoo! has evolved into a highly effective and valuable search engine.

This list-based approach is still quite obvious when looking Yahoo! Figure 4.1 is taken from the Yahoo! front page showing the top-level subject headings. These are:

- Arts and humanities
- Business and economy
- Computers and Internet
- Education
- Entertainment
- Government
- Health
- News and media
- Recreation and sports

Fig. 4.1   *The Yahoo! front page*

- Reference
- Regional
- Science
- Social science
- Society and culture.

Below these 14 major headings there are another 51 second level headings, and so on.

You can already see a major difference in the approach taken by Yahoo! (and indeed other index-based search engines) in that you can immediately see the type of information which is available. With a free text search engine it is necessary to run a search before being in a position to see the data the engine covers.

Human indexing rather than computer generation

A second major difference is that all of these headings and subheadings have been created by people; there is a much greater human input into index-based search engines than you will normally find with free text engines. This is both an advantage and a disadvantage. The advantage is that it is easier to work out the way in which another human being thinks than it is to second-guess a computer, so if you think of a subject, you can probably guess with a reasonable level of accuracy which of the major subject headings will cover that subject. The disadvantage is paradoxically the same; the success of an index based approach depends on the user thinking in the same way that the creator of the index does. If the creator of the index has a different bias (cultural or geographical, for example) you may spend a long time searching for your information in entirely the wrong place. I will go into this in more detail later in the chapter.

However, for now, let's look into Yahoo! in rather more detail. Clicking on any of the subheadings brings up another page which provides you with a further breakdown of the subject, and so on, until you finally reach a page which gives you a list of sites that you can click on. Figure 4.2 illustrates what happens when you click on the top-level heading 'Reference'. The numbers in brackets after each subheading indicate the total number of Web sites listed under that heading, and the @ sign indicates that the heading is also used elsewhere within the index, so it is possible to move between different subjects easily in order to find the information which you require. This is particularly the case with commercial categories, which are linked to their appropriate non-commercial counterparts.

This last point is an important one with respect to Yahoo!. When authors register their page(s) with the search engine, they can choose up to two categories within which to list the page, and if it is a commercial site, it must be placed under a commercial section. You should take this into account whenusing the engine. To use the example given by Yahoo!, if you have an interest in baseball cards, sites which cover this subject can be found in two places:

- Business and Economy: Companies: Sports: Collectibles: Cards: Baseball
- Recreation: Sports: Baseball: Collectibles: Baseball Cards: Commercial@

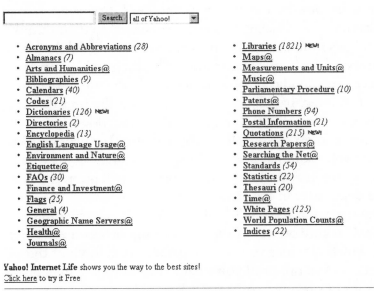

- Acronyms and Abbreviations *(28)*
- Almanacs *(7)*
- Arts and Humanities@
- Bibliographies *(9)*
- Calendars *(40)*
- Codes *(21)*
- Dictionaries *(126)* NEW!
- Directories *(2)*
- Encyclopedia *(13)*
- English Language Usage@
- Environment and Nature@
- Etiquette@
- FAQs *(30)*
- Finance and Investment@
- Flags *(25)*
- General *(4)*
- Geographic Name Servers@
- Health@
- Journals@
- Libraries *(1821)* NEW!
- Maps@
- Measurements and Units@
- Music@
- Parliamentary Procedure *(10)*
- Patents@
- Phone Numbers *(94)*
- Postal Information *(21)*
- Quotations *(215)* NEW!
- Research Papers@
- Searching the Net@
- Standards *(54)*
- Statistics *(22)*
- Thesauri *(20)*
- Time@
- White Pages *(125)*
- World Population Counts@
- Indices *(22)*

Yahoo! Internet Life shows you the way to the best sites!
Click here to try it Free

Fig. 4.2 *Yahoo! subheadings below the top-level 'Reference' heading*

and these two categories are linked.

This also works for regions of the world, and is an area that can cause some confusion. If you have an interest in the British General Election of 1997, the most sensible place to begin your search may at first glance appear to be under the Government: Politics hierarchy. However, because this is specific to a single region (i.e. the United Kingdom), it is necessary to look under the Regional heading – Regional: Countries: United_Kingdom: Government: Politics: Elections: 1997_General_Election. The Government: Politics hierarchy immediately takes you into information on the American political system.

If a Web site is in any way regional, Yahoo! will always place it in the appropriate regional category, rather than directly into a main subject category, and the only time this rule is superseded is when a subject or an organization is global in nature. In most cases you will need to remember to check under the appropriate regional heading, although in most instances Yahoo! will also cross-reference directly to the subject area as well.

The basic approach to using Yahoo! is therefore quite simple: decide which major heading your subject comes under, and follow the links through the hierarchy until you reach it. As a result of this simplicity it is a very good search engine to direct novice searchers towards, and as long as they are made aware of some of the idiosyncrasies of the system they should be able to retrieve good results quickly.

Advanced searching in Yahoo!

If you refer back to Figure 4.1 you will notice that there is a search box, which sits above the subject listing. This can be used to save a lot of time, as some of the hierarchies are quite deep (the general election example above goes down seven levels, for example) and it can be quite a time consuming task to click on a heading, wait for the page to load, click on the next and so on. A faster and more effective approach is to make use of the search box. You can input your search here, and Yahoo! will present you with two sets of responses, the first being any categories which use the word or phrase you have entered, and the second being actual Web sites that also contain the requested words.

This is very useful for a number of reasons:

■ The returned list of categories allows you to identify quickly the precise section of the hierarchy which is appropriate.
■ You can go directly to the category without going through the process of clicking on a seemingly endless series of headings.
■ The whole process can be circumnavigated by going directly to one of the Web sites listed.

Figure 4.3 gives an example of how this works in practice, when I did a search on diabetes, but which excluded children. Figure 4.4 is a portion of the results which were returned to me.

You can see from the search that I made use of the + symbol to include the particular word that I wanted, together with the - symbol to exclude references to children (I should also have excluded terms such as juvenile). Yahoo! includes some of the common operator symbols, such as we have already seen in operation at AltaVista, but it also has some others, such as t:<text> to search in the title of a document, or u:<text> to search in a URL. Yahoo! also allows phrase searching with double quotes (" "), and wildcard matching using the ★ symbol. Next to the search box is a link to allow you to choose specific options, such as running an exact phrase search, an AND or OR search, a search for a person's name, to retrieve pages from a particular time period, or to search in one of the four major categories outlined below. Of these, the last three are of most value, since the 'subject category' choice can simply be run in the search box itself using the switches already outlined.

+diabetes -children   Search options

Fig. 4.3   *Using the search option in Yahoo! to look for diabetes, but not children*

When Yahoo! does a search of this type, it searches through the four areas of its database as follows:

- subject categories
- Web sites
- Net events and chat
- recent news articles.

If Yahoo! is unable to find any sites or categories which match the search, it will automatically pass on the search request to AltaVista and return any results. It therefore makes sense to make use of the syntax which AltaVista understands, in order to get a tightly focused set of results.

In the diabetes example, I was returned a total of 16 categories and 313 Web sites that matched my criteria, which therefore enabled me quickly to decide where to go next. In many ways this is a more helpful approach than we find with AltaVista if you know little about the subject, since the categories returned give you a very clear idea of what is actually available within that general subject area.

Yahoo! ranks the Web pages it finds using its own set of algorithms:

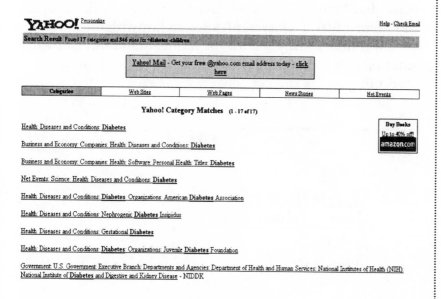

Fig. 4.4   *Partial results of the diabetes search*

HINTS AND TIPS
Search engines rank their results according to their own criteria, so the same search will result in a different set of results on different search engines.

■ Multiple keywords. Any document which contains all of your keywords is ranked higher than one which contains fewer of them.

■ Title words. Any words found in the title are weighted as being more important than those which only occur in the body of the text or in the URL.

■ Category. More general category matches are placed before more specific matches.

Yahoo! does, however, go further than this, since you can also do a search within a specific subject area. There are times when you may be quite clear on the particular approach you wish to take to a specific subject, but even when the search has been narrowed down using the hierarchical structure there may still be many hundreds or indeed thousands of Web sites available. It is possible to limit a Yahoo! search to a specific category; when you navigate through the hierarchy Yahoo! always displays a search box similar to the one we have already seen in Figure 4.3, but it includes an option to search just within the current category, as Figure 4.5 illustrates.

An interest in the Star Trek spacecraft *USS Enterprise* will, in all probability, give me far too many hits if I do a general search in Yahoo!, but by narrowing myself down into the News and Media: Television: Genres: Science fiction, fantasy and horror: Star Trek section, a search just within this category will substantially reduce the number of results and will automatically focus on that one area, instead of finding everything on the subject.

| "USS Enterprise" | Search | just this category ▼ |

- **Episode Guides** *(9)*
- **General Information**@
- **Scripts** *(4)*
- **Soundtracks**@

Fig. 4.5 *A subject-specific search in a Yahoo! category*

As you can see, Yahoo! is not a difficult search engine to use; in fact it is very straightforward. However, the value in using it does not only rest on its simplicity, but also on the fact that it has a number of other very useful features as well. Yahoo!, in common with other major search engines, is always attempting to broaden its user base, and as a result has a regular programme of updating and adding new features. Some of these have little relevance to us as searchers, but others can prove quite useful. If you return to look at Figure 4.1 for a moment you will see that there are a number of icons at the top of the screen, and below the search box is another series of links. I'll briefly go through these features, and highlight those which have particular value to searchers.

- *What's New*. Here you can find details on new additions to the database, current events information, events which are taking place on the Internet on a particular day, and also daily entertainment. It is a useful section if you simply want to get a quick overview of what is happening today, but because of its very nature you will find information more by luck than judgement.
- *Today's News*. This section provides links into top news stories in areas such as Business, Technical, Politics, World, Entertainment and so on.
- *More Yahoos*. This section links into World Yahoo!s and Metro Yahoo!s. These can be very useful for particular regions, and are discussed in detail below.
- *Yellow Pages*. If you need to find a business within a particular area of the USA this simple search engine will return a list of businesses which match the given criteria.
- *People Search*. Yahoo! provides a facility to search for individuals with a link into another search engine, Four11. People search engines are discussed in more detail in Chapter 5.
- *Maps*. This section is again useful if you need to find a particular location in the USA, and it can also provide useful information on travelling to a location.
- *My Yahoo!* is discussed in detail in Chapter 8 on intelligent agents
- *Sports, Weather, Chat, Email, Personals, Shopping, Classifieds*

are all self-explanatory and have little direct relevance to the searcher.

Regional Yahoo!s

Earlier I mentioned that one problem with Yahoo! is that in order to find information on a particular region, it is necessary to drill down through the Regional heading to reach the data that you are interested in. Yahoo! has approached this problem by providing World and Metro Yahoo!s. They are continually adding new ones to their service, so there is little point in trying to list those that they currently have; I would simply suggest that you visit Yahoo! yourself and click on the 'More Yahoo!s' link. I will, however, spend a little time looking at the UK & Ireland version, to illustrate the difference between the main engine and the regional ones. This version can be reached by clicking on the link from the main Yahoo! home page, or by going to **http://www.yahoo.co.uk.**

As you can see from a comparison of Figures 4.1 and 4.6, there is very little difference between the two indexes; both have the same physical appearance, and both work in exactly the same way, with broadly the same options. There are some slight differences, however – with the global version, there is a link to Yahoo! Yellow Pages, but in the UK & Ireland version you will find a UK Business Directory instead.

There are some larger differences when you inspect the major subject headings. For example, in the global version we find:

Government
Military, Politics, Law, Taxes

and in the UK & Ireland version we have:

Government
UK, Ireland, Europe, Politics

which does reflect an appropriately different emphasis. The observant searcher will also notice differences when drilling down into the hierarchy. Users of a regional Yahoo! can

Mink Farm Raid
Yahoo! Finance

AMSTERDAM £42.20 return

Yahoo! Football
US Embassy Bombings

[Search box] [Search] Options

Search: ⊙ All sites ○ UK & Ireland sites only

Accommodation - Football - Email Search - News - Stock Quotes - Pager - **Sport**
My Yahoo! - Weather - Yahoo! Mail - Yahoo! UK Business Directory - more

- **Arts and Humanities**
  Photography, Theatre, Literature

- **Business and Economy** [Xtra!]
  Companies, Investments, Classifieds, Taxes

- **Computers and Internet**
  Internet, WWW, Software, Multimedia

- **Education**
  UK, Ireland, Universities

- **Entertainment**
  Humour, Movies, Music

- **Government**
  UK, Ireland, Europe, Politics

- **Health**
  Medicine, Drugs, Diseases, Fitness

- **News and Media** [Xtra!]
  UK, Ireland, Magazines, Papers, TV

- **Recreation and Sport** [Xtra!]
  Sport, Outdoors, Travel, Motoring

- **Reference**
  Libraries, Dictionaries, Phone Numbers

- **Regional**
  UK, Ireland, Countries, Regions

- **Science**
  CS, Biology, Astronomy, Engineering

- **Social Science**
  Anthropology, Sociology, Economics

- **Society and Culture**
  People, Environment, Royalty, Religion

Fig. 4.6   *UK & Ireland Yahoo! home page*

choose to search either the entire database (which is the same as running the search on the global version), or to choose to search in the UK categories, for example. This is essentially the same as choosing the appropriate regional category from the global Yahoo!, but it is a rather faster route through to the same information. Even if you decide not to follow the UK route, once you have drilled far enough down into the category, the first sites which are displayed will be those which have a regional importance.

This can best be illustrated by looking at the category of Reference Libraries in both the global version (Figure 4.7) and the UK & Ireland version (Figure 4.8).

HINTS AND TIPS

If you want a geographic search, use a local version of Yahoo!, but if you want a comprehensive view, make use of the main version.

- Law Libraries@
- Lesbian, Gay and Bisexual@
- Library and Information Science *(223)*
- Literature@
- Map Libraries@
- Masonic Libraries@

- Sports Libraries@
- Theology Libraries@
- Transportation Libraries@
- U.S. State Libraries *(47)* NEW!
- Indices *(16)*

- Annual Reports Library - includes reports from corporations, foundations, banks, mutual funds and public institutions from around the world
- Australian Embassy Library, Jakarta - information about Australia and cultural events in Indonesia
- BIS Reference and Library Enquiry Service - British Information Services provides online information on all aspects of Britain to residents of the USA
- Coolib - featuring the Cool Library of the week. Nominations always welcome
- Corporate Intranets & Corporate Libraries - an investigation into the role that corporate libraries play in providing and disseminating information using the corporate intranet. An honours thesis by Alyn Jones
- French Library and Cultural Center - devoted to promoting the culture and language of France and the Francophone world
- Funding Information Center - a free, self-service library of research materials on grants, fundraising, and nonprofit management
- Henry Miller Library - in Big Sur, CA. Peruse rare books by Miller, an online bookstore, an art gallery, interactive forums and more
- Huntington Library@
- Kaapelisolmu - the Knot at the Cable - a pilot project in the field of equal access to electronic information, an electronic publishing house for the non-governmental organisations, cultural movements and individuals
- Karpeles Manuscript Library
- Libraries Online! - an initiative of the Microsoft Corporation, the American Library Association (ALA), and the Technology Resource Institute to research and develop innovative approaches for extending information technologies to underserved communities
- Library Company of Philadelphia - independent research library and museum with collections documenting the history and background of American culture from the colonial period to the end of the 19th century
- Mechanics' Institute Library - general interest membership library and chess club
- Meditating on the Library as Archive. From Alexandria to the Internet
- National Archives and Records Administration@
- National Library Week *(2)*
- PALS *(2)*

Fig. 4.7 *The global Yahoo! section for Reference Libraries, including headings and links to Web sites*

You can see that substantially there is very little difference; both versions have subheadings for Law Libraries@, Lesbian, Gay and Bisexual@, and Library and Information Science, for example. However, once we look at the sites which are returned in this category, the global version displays a simple alphabetical list of sites, while the UK & Ireland version begins with sites that are appropriate to both countries, indicating this with the use of small flags.

Consequently, there can be particular advantages to searching in a regional version of Yahoo!, rather than in the global version:

- Subjects appropriate to a region or country can be located more quickly.
- It is less confusing for novices to use.
- Appropriate Web sites are given greater prominence.
- Fewer matches are returned.

Yahoo! summary

Yahoo! is not a search engine in the strict sense of the term – it is a hierarchical index of Web sites. As authors of Web pages have to submit sites to Yahoo! (the engine does not employ a spider or robot utility), Yahoo! will retrieve a smaller set of results than some other engines, but those

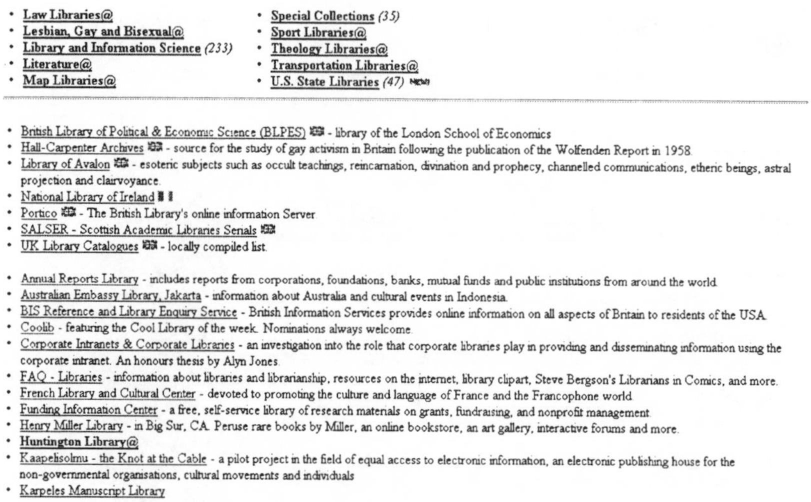

- Law Libraries@
- Lesbian, Gay and Bisexual@
- Library and Information Science (233)
- Literature@
- Map Libraries@

- Special Collections (35)
- Sport Libraries@
- Theology Libraries@
- Transportation Libraries@
- U.S. State Libraries (47) NEW!

- British Library of Political & Economic Science (BLPES) 🔲 - library of the London School of Economics
- Hall-Carpenter Archives 🔲 - source for the study of gay activism in Britain following the publication of the Wolfenden Report in 1958.
- Library of Avalon 🔲 - esoteric subjects such as occult teachings, reincarnation, divination and prophecy, channelled communications, etheric beings, astral projection and clairvoyance.
- National Library of Ireland 🔲 🔲
- Portico 🔲 - The British Library's online information Server
- SALSER - Scottish Academic Libraries Serials 🔲
- UK Library Catalogues 🔲 - locally compiled list.

- Annual Reports Library - includes reports from corporations, foundations, banks, mutual funds and public institutions from around the world.
- Australian Embassy Library, Jakarta - information about Australia and cultural events in Indonesia.
- BIS Reference and Library Enquiry Service - British Information Services provides online information on all aspects of Britain to residents of the USA.
- Coolib - featuring the Cool Library of the week. Nominations always welcome.
- Corporate Intranets & Corporate Libraries - an investigation into the role that corporate libraries play in providing and disseminating information using the corporate intranet. An honours thesis by Alyn Jones.
- FAQ - Libraries - information about libraries and librarianship, resources on the internet, library clipart, Steve Bergson's Librarians in Comics, and more.
- French Library and Cultural Center - devoted to promoting the culture and language of France and the Francophone world.
- Funding Information Center - a free, self-service library of research materials on grants, fundraising, and nonprofit management.
- Henry Miller Library - in Big Sur, CA. Peruse rare books by Miller, an online bookstore, an art gallery, interactive forums and more.
- Huntington Library@
- Kaapelisolmu - the Knot at the Cable - a pilot project in the field of equal access to electronic information, an electronic publishing house for the non-governmental organisations, cultural movements and individuals
- Karpeles Manuscript Library

Fig. 4.8 *The UK & Ireland Yahoo! section for Reference Libraries, including headings and links to Web sites*

results will generally be very tightly focused. It is possible to find appropriate sites quickly with only the smallest amount of information about the subject being researched, and the structure of the engine provides an excellent overview of a particular subject.

Other index-based search engines

The structure of Yahoo! is very appealing, both for organizations establishing Web search engines and also for those people who are new to searching. Consequently, it is an approach which is becoming more widely used. As we have already seen, traditional free text search engines are now beginning to incorporate a directory structure, and it is becoming more difficult to classify search engines into different types. However, there are a number of other search engines which have their historical roots based firmly in the directory structure, and I'll point out some others which you may wish to look at, in much the same way that I did with free text search engines.

Magellan

The Magellan home page at **http://www.mckinley.com** is shown in Figure 4.9

As you can see, both Magellan and Yahoo! use the same

Fig. 4.9 *The Magellan Internet Guide*

basic approach of broad subject headings with narrower sub-headings below, but while the basic structure is the same, Magellan has a number of different features. You can search using the hierarchical approach, but it is also possible to search the 60,000 sites which have been reviewed, although the reviews seem to be descriptive rather than analytical. An interesting feature are the 'Green light sites'; these sites have been checked and those which have 'adult' content have been screened out, ensuring that users will have no nasty surprises when they click on links.

Magellan allows for 'advanced searching', which simply allows you to make use of the usual '+', '-' and " " for phrase searching.

Net Find, G.O.D. and Snap

Three other sites, all very similar in concept and approach are Net Find at **http://www.net-find.com**, the Global Online Directory at **http://www.god.co.uk**, and Snap at **http://www.snap.com**. Since they are alike I have just listed the different major categories that they use below.

Net Find

Business	Computers	Culture	Directories
Discover	Fun stuff	Living	Music
The Net	News	Online Reading	References
Shopping	Showbiz	Sports	Spotlight
Travel	Web Master		

G.O.D.

Arts/Crafts	Business	Community	Entertainment
Finance	Games	Finance	Internet
Hot and Sexy	Internet	Leisure	Paranormal
Personal pages	Sports	Technical	Travel

Snap

Arts	Business	Computers	Education
Entertainment	Health	Kids and Family	Living
Local	News	Oddities	People
Science	Shopping	Sport	Travel

This nicely illustrates that many of the index based search engines are designed for rather more generalized and recreational uses, rather than academic or work-related use. None of them approaches the depth of coverage provided by Yahoo! though this does not of course invalidate their use and value in certain situations.

Other index-based search engines
Galaxy Tradewave: **http://galaxy.tradewave.com**
No Search: **http://www.nosearch.com**

Summary
Index based search engines provide users with a straightforward approach to finding information by guiding them through a series of headings and subheadings until they are able to locate the information that they require. As a result they are very useful if you need to obtain an overview of a subject, or if you have a limited amount of knowledge about a subject. While all engines of this type provide headings, some are more in-depth than others, and your choice of engine should take this into account.

URLs mentioned in this chapter

http://www.yahoo.com
http://www.yahoo.co.uk
http://www.mckinley.com
http://www.net-find.com
http://www.god.co.uk
http://www.snap.com.
http://galaxy.tradewave.com
http://www.nosearch.com

5

Multi-search engines and more!

Introduction

We have now looked at a variety of different search engines, and it is worth emphasizing that they make up a very small percentage of the total number that are available. Each of them has its own strengths and weaknesses, and you will have discovered that you may need to use several of them to be confident that you have found everything that you need. This can be a time consuming and frustrating experience, since you will often find references to exactly the same site from a number of different engines.

However, there is a solution to this problem, which is to make use of multi- or meta-search engines. This chapter concentrates on explaining what multi-search engines do and the different types. In common with the previous chapters, I take an in-depth look at one in particular.

What is a multi-search engine?

As the name implies, it is an engine that searches across multiple search engines on your behalf, displaying records on the screen in any one of a number of different formats. There are a variety of types of multi-search engine available, with their own strengths and weaknesses.

The simplest form is not really a multi-search engine at all, but simply a collection of links to different search engines, which may or may not include a dialog box to enable you to input search terms. Once the search has been input, you will be taken directly to the chosen search engine's home page to view the results.

The second type of multi-search engine allows you to input your search into a single dialog box, and in some cases to choose the search engines you want to be interrogated.

The multi-search engine will passes the query onto the chosen engines and displays the results, usually arranged in order of search engine.

The final type of multi-search engine is rather more sophisticated – it does all that the previous type does, but then de-duplicates the records to remove sites which are mentioned twice or more, and attempts to sort all the records into a more useful order.

As each of these multi-search engines takes a different approach, let's look at them a little more closely.

Lists of search engines

As I have already mentioned, a multi-search engine of this type does not actually do any searching, but simply displays a list of other engines that can be used. At first thought this does not appear to be particularly valuable, but in fact this approach can bring many more search engines to your attention than you would otherwise have been aware of. A good example of this is the Metaplus multi-search engine, shown in Figure 5.1, which can be found on the Web at **http://www.metaplus.com**. Just looking at the area of health, Metaplus lists over 50 different search engines that you can jump to and begin searching. Metaplus has a separate section on the UK, which runs to several hundred different resources that may be of use.

Consequently, search engines of this type can provide you with many valuable starting points in areas that are new to you, or about which you only have only limited basic knowledge.

Consecutive multi-search engines

To be faced with such a bewildering array of search engines can be somewhat daunting, particularly if you have to choose one of them based on little more than its name and the heading it is to be found under. Considerable time can be spent simply going to one engine, running a search, returning to the list and trying another. The consecutive multi-search engines overcome that problem by allowing you to run the search in one go. A good example of this type of engine is the Internet Sleuth at **http://www.isleuth.com**. Figure 5.2 illustrates the dialog box used to input the search term(s) and

metaplus

headlines
business
media

Home	Library
HOME	LookUp
Topics	Mzines
Acad.	Mrkting
Art	Media
Biz	Music
Books	Navig.
Cars	NEWS
Cities	Pets
cGames	Politics
Dance	Publish
Drink	Radio
eComm	Search
Edu	Shops
EdTech	Sports
Fashion	TechNs
Film	Theatre
Food	Transp.
Gov.	Travel
Health	TV
Hobbies	UK
Internet	WallSt
Invest	Wealth
Jobs	World
Kids	Writers
Law	Finally!

directories
plus
essential
sites

Search

| Home |

■ **Search**

Lists	The Engines	NorthernLight	Databases	News
The-Word	Alta Vista	OneKey	Direct Search	Only
Tools	Anzwers	Pinstripe	Internets	News Index
Windweaver	Excite	Search.com	European	Usenet
Multiple	HotBot	Sleuth	Search	DejaNews
Search	Info Seek	Thunderstone	sites	Engine
Beaucoup	Lycos	Web Crawler	EuroSeek	Info
FindSpot	MetaCrawler	Yahoo!	YellowWeb	SEwatch

■ **Search for...**

Specific	Digital Imaging	Law	Sports	Internet info.
Searching	Drugs	Marketing	StudyAbroad	NetSearcher
Aviation	Energy	Music	Trademarks	Seniors'
BooksOnline	Finance	Mythology	UK Media	FreeStuff
BookReviews	GradSchools	People	U.S.Gov.Info	Software dev.
Businesses	FemaleHealth	Quotations	Video Games	devSEARCH
Clip Art	Healthfinder	Shakespeare	Water-related	Worldwide
Colleges	Humor	Shops	Women	eDirectory
Craft/Hobby	Industry	Small Biz	1980s	World Trade

■ **Related Topics on Metaplus and other links**

Libraries - browse, search world libraries + Digital Librarian
LookUp - businesses + people + telephone nos. + email addresses
Web Navigation - web directories + quick ref sites
Language problems? Try AltaVista Translations
Access categories from original Metaplus big pages via left hand columns

© Technology Relations 1997-98. Site maintained by: John Lewell

Fig. 5.1   *The Metaplus pages for the Search and Search for . . .
options*

to decide which engines to use.

In the search illustrated, I asked the Internet Sleuth to run a search for 'intelligent agents' across AltaVista, Excite and Infoseek, and to spend a maximum of one minute on it. The search was passed across to the search engines, and when they responded, the Internet Sleuth compiled the results onto another page for me, displaying the results from each search engine in turn.

The advantage of this approach is quite obvious – it saved me considerable time. The results were exactly the same as running separate searches, but they were brought to me at the Internet Sleuth site, so I did not have to wander around the Web to each search engine in turn. Unfortunately, however, there are a number of disadvantages to this approach as well:

■ Not all search engines use the same search syntax, and while AltaVista understands that placing words into dou-

HINTS AND TIPS
Remember that not all search engines use the same syntax, so limit your search to single words, or use + and - which are the two most common ways of limiting the search. However, even with these you should check to ensure that the search engines you choose will accept their use.

Fig. 5.2 *The Internet Sleuth main search page*

ble quotes means that you wish to do a phrase search, other engines which do not use that syntax may interpret your search as being for separate words – or they may not run the search at all. Therefore, you need to have a good understanding of each of the engines you choose to use in this situation, or you are limited to the lowest common denominator, which is a list of single words.

- A second problem is that at busy times some search engines will need to take longer to run the query than the time limit set by the Internet Sleuth, which means that you will only get partial results, or none at all. Other multi-search engines, which do not provide a maximum search-time parameter, run the risk of forcing you to wait until all the results are available before displaying them on the screen, thus losing the time advantage which is otherwise inherent in this approach.

- The final problem is that, since each search engine is working independently of the others, you may well find exactly the same set of results displayed by each search engine. This causes you to waste time trying to find unique records from a mass of duplicates.

Advanced multi-search engines

A new breed of multi-search engines have recently arrived on the Web; they overcome many of these problems. They provide you with a variety of search engines on which you can run your search, but they will interpret the results for you and will do their best to remove duplicates and put them

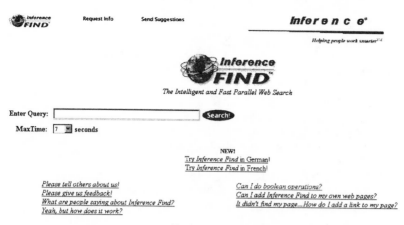

Fig. 5.3   *Inference Find home page*

into a sensible order.

One of the best examples of this type of multi-search engine is Inference Find, which is available at **http://www. infind.com/**. Its home page can be seen in Figure 5.3. This engine calls in parallel to WebCrawler, Yahoo!, Lycos, AltaVista, InfoSeek and Excite, although the search engines used can be customized. In some instances it will make several calls to the same search engine if that engine only returns ten hits at a time. By repeating the search, Inference Find is able to produce a large number of results; other multi-search engines may well just take the first ten results returned, thus reducing their comprehensiveness. The results will then be merged and displayed in under category headings. An example of this can be seen in Figure 5.4, which shows some of the results returned from a search for 'intelligent agents'. Inference Find grouped the results together under headings such as 'Misc. educational institution sites', 'Misc. commercial', 'Intelligent software agents', 'Misc. European sites' and so on. It obviously makes use of the URLs of the different hosts in order to create these groupings, and so may return a site under the heading of 'Misc. European commercial sites' even though the page actually refers to information about the USA for example. Nonetheless, the groupings can still be of considerable use, as they allow you to differentiate between commercial sites relating to a film or television series and those produced by fans, for example.

- PAAM'96
- Self Clustering Intelligent Agents.

Software Agents

- AgentBuilder
- Amazon Bookstore Resources - Software Agents
- CyberAgents Group
- Intelligent Agents - Software Agents Net Links
- MIT Media Lab - Software Agents Group
- More Timely Resources - Software Agents
- Research and Documentation - Software Agents Net Links
- Software agents are intelligent on-line assistants

Intelligent Software Agents

- Intelligent Software Agents
- Intelligent Software Agents
- Intelligent Software Agents
- Intelligent Software Agents - Carnegie Mellon University
- Intelligent Software Agents in Practise - Summary

Misc. Commercial Sites

- Associative Cognition, Inc. Ships Prody Parrot(TM)
- Benjamin Grosof's biography and background
- Cetus Links: 9556 Links on Objects and Components / Mobile A...
- Fortean Times Reviews: The X-Files Movie - FT114
- NetWatch Top Ten Links
- Spain's Telefonica To Expand Its Use of Summa Four Switches With New V...

Fig. 5.4   *Partial list of results from Inference Find for the search for 'intelligent agents'*

An in-depth look at the Internet Sleuth

Having looked in general terms at the types of multi–search engines available, I'll now concentrate on one in particular to give you an in–depth understanding of the ways in which these engines can be used to best effect. I briefly mentioned the Internet Sleuth earlier, and now return to it since it is one of the most powerful of the multi–search engines, even though it is perhaps not as sophisticated in some ways as Inference Find.

The Internet Sleuth provides you with six major types of search, linking into different search engines as necessary. The example in Figure 5.2 shows the dialog box for a search using Web search engines and directories, allowing you to choose

DID YOU KNOW?

Ever wondered what everyone is actually searching for? Visit http://www.metaspy.com to see the search terms people use. There is a filtered and an unfiltered link, which is updated every 15 seconds.

up to six engines from a list of AltaVista, Excite, Infoseek, Lycos, WebCrawler and Yahoo!. However, it also has the ability to focus searches in a number of other areas:

- Web reviewed sites
- What's new?
- News
- Business and finance
- Software
- Usenet news groups.

In each category the Sleuth provides you with a choice of appropriate search engines. This makes searching much easier, and provides access to search engines that you may never have heard of before.

Of course, this is useful, but not outstanding. Where the Internet Sleuth becomes particularly valuable is in the total number of databases to which it provides access.

The left-hand side of the main screen provides the user with a search box and a list of categories, ranging from Arts to Veterinary/Zoological. The category list is similar in approach to that found with Yahoo!, in that each subject area can be further subdivided to produce narrower and more focused subject headings. 'Regional' is broken down into the following subheadings:

Africa
Asia
Australia and Oceania
Canada
Caribbean, C&S America
Europe
   United Kingdom
Middle East
United States
   (16 individual states listed under this heading)

When you click on a heading or subheading, the Sleuth presents a list of search engines on the right-hand side of the screen which match the subject coverage on the left.

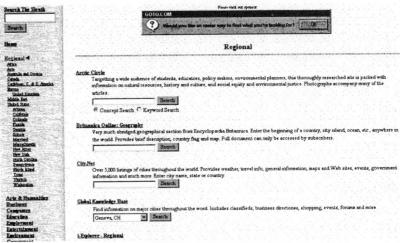

Fig. 5.5   *Partial list of Internet Sleuth regional search engines*

Continuing to use the same example, clicking on 'Regional' produces a list of search engines which includes Arctic Circle, Britannica Online, City.Net, Global Knowledge Base, i-Explorer and several others. As a result, appropriate search engines can be identified quickly and easily, and are searchable directly from the Sleuth. Links are also given to allow the user to jump directly to the home page of the search engine they are interested in. This can be seen in Figure 5.5.

If you are uncertain as to which is the most appropriate search engine to use, you can use the small search box 'Search the Sleuth' in the top left-hand corner of the screen. This searches through the names and descriptions of search engines available at the site in order to locate ones that cover your area of interest. Consequently this should be used to search for general, rather than specific, terms. The Sleuth will not turn up any matches if you search for your favourite soccer team, but it will give a number of hits if you search for the more general term 'soccer'.

Single-site search engines

The difference between a single-site search engine and the search engines that we have talked about so far should be reasonably obvious – a single-site engine will search a site, a specific resource, or a particular database. What may be less than obvious, however, is that quite often the only way of finding information in a particular database will be to use its own specific search engine; general search engines will not work in this instance. AltaVista and the other engines previously mentioned are able to search Web pages or newsgroups, but they are unable to get into databases and index them, either because the database is password-protected, or more often because the data is not held in a format that the search engines can work with.

The single-site engines have been written in such a way that they can interrogate their own database(s) and return the data to the user on a Web page created 'on the fly', which is to say on a page specifically made for the user. The page is only created as a result of the query, and as soon as the user leaves the page it ceases to exist. For this reason it is not possible for general Web search engines to index the data, since it is not stored in a form that they can access.

There is no standard format for these single-site search engines, since they are written to perform specific tasks. I've provided three examples below.

Figure 5.6 is a screenshot from a search engine designed to

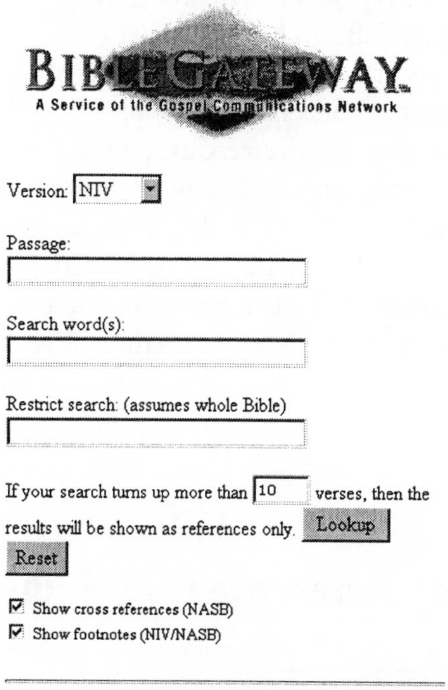

Fig. 5.6   *Searching the Bible at the Bible Gateway*
(Copyright Gospel Communications Network (GCN) A Ministry of Gospel Communications International, Inc. – The 21st Century Gospel Films)

Hypertext Webster Gateway

Enter word here:
Exact ⊙ Approx ○

Look up definition   Clear entry

Figure 5.7 *The search interface for Webster's dictionary*

search the Bible, which can be found at **http://bible.gospelcom.net/**. This allows you to decide which version should be searched, and whether to look for a particular passage, or to search for a word or phrase.

The Bible search engine is obviously not appropriate for searching a straightforward dictionary, so Webster's dictionary **http://work.ucsd.edu:5141/cgi–bin/http_webster** provides an entirely different interface (see Figure 5.7).

Both of these search engines differ from that provided by the Internet Public Library at **http://www.ipl.org/ref/Search.html**, shown in Figure 5.8.

It should come as no surprise that the output from each of these search engines is also quite different.

It is worth exploring some of these site/resource specific search engines for yourself, as they are obviously the most focused search engines available on the Web. Unfortunately, there is no single comprehensive source for them, because they are so specific, but the Internet Sleuth provides the best listing that I have discovered, with the Metaplus site a close second.

◆the Internet Public Library

Search the IPL Ready Reference Collection

Search Terms:

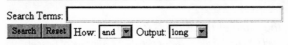

Search   Reset   How: and ▾   Output: long ▾

Fig. 5.8   *The search interface for the IPL ready reference collection*

People searchers

Before leaving the subject of search engines, there is a final very useful type that deserves mention. I'm often asked for the best method of locating an individual, and I would generally start such a search by looking in AltaVista for the individual's name, either as a phrase search or using adjacency with the near operator. If that person has a Web site, or they are referred to on one, that will usually locate them. If that fails, my next attempt would be to check Deja News to see if they have posted to any newsgroups. My final approach, if both of these have failed, is to try one of the many people searchers available on the Web.

A people searcher does exactly what you would imagine; it tries to track down individuals given only a small amount of information. There are a number of these available, and both AltaVista and Yahoo! provide links from their home pages to people searchers. I tend to make use of two in particular – Four11 at **http://www.four11.com** and Bigfoot at **http://www.bigfoot.com**; both are reasonably comprehensive. Four11 has over 15 million names in its database, which it has obtained using voluntary registration (which accounts for 4 million), automatic registration by internet service providers, and public sources such as newsgroups. Both allow casual users to search them for names, but in order to increase the size of their databases extra facilities are available if you register with them, providing them with details about yourself. Figure 5.9 illustrates the search screen at Four11, which is simplicity itself to fill in; you just need to give first name and surname, together with any further information you have available. The results are restricted to a maximum of 50 hits if you are an unregistered user, or 200 if you have registered. Four11 also allows registered members to search on and display a number of other criteria, such as previous e-mail addresses, their organization, interests, hobbies, educational institutions and so on. If the person being searched for is based in the USA, Four11 will attempt to locate a telephone number as well. I ran a search for 'Phil Bradley' and got a total of 42 possible matches, including the correct one.

Bigfoot gave me almost as many hits when I ran the same search using their search engine; Figure 5.10 displays their

HINTS AND TIPS

Remember that some people use shortened versions of their names or nicknames, so run searches which match Phil and Philip for example whenever the search engine gives you that opportunity.

Four**11** the internet white pages   by YAHOO!

Directories
· White Pages
· Yellow Pages
· Maps
· Net Phone

Information
· Free E-Mail
· Help/FAQ
· Advertising

We Speak
English ▾
Go!

White Pages

E-Mail Search   Advanced E-mail Search

First Name   Last Name
[   ]   [   ]   Search

Domain
[   ]   ☑ SmartName (Bob=Robert)   Clear

Find an old friend or lost relative!
Phone Number Search

Enter at least the **last name** of the person you're searching for:

First Name   Last Name
[   ]   [   ]   Search

City   State
[   ]   [ ] (2-letter abbreviation) Clear

1994 - 1998 Yahoo! Corp., All Rights Reserved

Fig. 5.9   *The Four11 interface enabling you to search for long-lost friends, colleagues or second cousins twice removed*

home page. You can see both people searchers also provide access to Yellow Pages, so it is possible to run searches for companies and organizations as well as individuals.

Bigfoot.com "Your Internet Is Served"

Join Bigfoot - FREE
Search Bigfoot
Member's Entrance
FEETures
Support Center

Bigfoot is proud to help bring all netizens together, one search at a time.

Customize your **E-mail** in ways you've only dreamed! **FREE**

AirMedia Live

Search Bigfoot
👤 People 🌐 Web Pages 📖 Yellow Pages

☑ E-mail ☐ White Page
Search Ex : John Smith
[   ]
                    Search

Fig. 5.10 *The Bigfoot search interface*

Summary

In this chapter I have gone into some detail about how the last major group of search engines work, although, as we shall see in the next chapter, there is still more to learn in this area. Multi-search engines provide you with access to a wide variety of engines, allowing you to do a more wide-ranging and comprehensive search than is possible with a single search engine, but at the expense of the sophistication now inherent in some of the more advanced engines.

Single-site or resource-specific search engines have a very focused approach, dealing with a specific topic or database of information. What they may miss in terms of advanced search methods they can more than make up for in providing you with a very small number of relevant hits, thereby saving you time in the long run.

URLs mentioned in this chapter

http://www.metaplus.com
http://www.isleuth.com
http://www.infind.com/
http://www.metaspy.com
http://bible.gospelcom.net/
http://work.ucsd.edu:5141/cgi-bin/http_webster
http://www.ipl.org/ref/Search.html
http://www.four11.com
http://www.bigfoot.com

6

Other available database resources

Introduction

Given the size of the Internet and the size of this book, it is not going to be possible to list every information resource that is available to the advanced searcher, or even to go into detail about what is available. However, I think it is important to try to point you towards as many different ways of obtaining information as I can, so this chapter brings together some of the other ways that you can find out information from Internet database resources.

Some of these are free resources, while others are ones that you have to subscribe to or pay for on a 'pay as you go' basis. It is important that we cover these, since it is all too easy to limit yourself to using material which has been made freely available. The advanced Internet searcher will, however be aware of a wide variety of Internet resources, and should at least consider the possibility of using commercial as well as free ones.

Some of the resources that I look at in this chapter are:

- information provided free of charge by publishers
- online communities
- commercial information
- online journals
- newspapers
- bookshops
- paid services offered by search engines.

Freely available information provided by publishers

It sounds a little bit too good to be true, doesn't it? However, most publishers are indeed offering free material on the Internet that you might well expect to have to pay for. You may rest assured that they have sound financial reasons for providing this information as a 'loss leader' – they hope that you will value the data enough to subscribe to the fully paid-up subscription-based service that they offer.

I'm aware that at this point I'm racing ahead a little bit, because I've started to talk about 'publishers' without fully explaining what I mean. This is because the term 'publisher' is becoming increasingly difficult to define clearly and neatly. In the 'old days', if I can refer to a situation which existed twenty years ago as 'old', a publisher was an organization which produced printed books or journals and then sold the result to you and me. With the arrival of online, this definition was expanded to include organizations (sometimes the same ones, but more often different organizations) which published in a digital format, first via large databases stored on mainframe computers, and then on optical discs, such as CD-ROM. The arrival of the Internet has made the definition much more difficult, since in a sense I 'publish' articles that I write directly onto my Web site, making me both author and publisher. Anyone who produces a Web site and makes information available from it can, with a certain amount of justification, be described as a publisher. However, for clarity I am using 'publisher' to refer to organizations which have previously made data available either in hard-copy form, or via an online database or in CD-ROM format.

These organizations are very keen to use the Internet, since it provides them with another means of making their data available, and so information professionals now have greater flexibility in deciding how to receive their data. I will return to this subject in Chapter 10, the information mix. All we need consider at the moment is the fact that one of the ways in which publishers are attracting customers is by offering data for nothing.

Each publisher provides different types of free information, and my first example is Kluwer Academic Publishers, at **http://www.wkap.nl/**. You can obtain a full listing of their titles, details about each, and sample copies of journals; you can also view their tables of contents and some articles. They are also currently (1998) offering institutional subscribers free, seamless full-text access to the Kluwer journals.

Sweet and Maxwell, a legal publisher with a Web site at **http://www.smlawpub.co.uk/**, offers a whole raft of free information, such as access to the solicitors' journal *Lawbrief*, *Kime's international law directory*, *The Bar directory* and several other publications.

My next example of the work being done by electronic publishers comes from Chadwyck-Healey at **http://www. chadwyck.co.uk**. In common with other electronic publishers, they are making their products available across the Internet, accessed via a subscription and password. Once one has purchased a subscription, one can search and retrieve data from any of the subscribed databases. However, the company is also attempting to add value to its products by creating a number of other subsidiary services. Chadwyck-Healey publishes widely in the field of literature and poetry, and they have a 'writer in residence' who chooses poems from their databases and provides commentaries on them. Visitors to the site are encouraged to become involved with this process by submitting their own poems, for example.

Creating an online community

Some companies create an online community based around an area of shared interest. An example of this can be seen at BioMedNet's site at **http://www.biomednet.com**. This is described as an 'online club for the biological and medical research community' and already has over 50,000 members. Membership is free upon registration, and this allows access to a library of full-text journals, biological databases, and the MEDLINE database, a job exchange, discussion groups, a shopping mall and a members' magazine. Members can search all the databases, but viewing the full text of articles from partner publishers usually requires a payment or subscription to the product.

Organizations subscribing to BioMedNet can place funds into a central account, or can allocate funds to individuals who can then fulfil their own information requirements. Individuals can also deposit funds into their own account by cheque or credit card.

As a result, users of the system are able to meet online and have discussions; they are informed about new developments in their areas of interest, notified about new publications, can search existing resources, download articles and generally keep in daily contact with professionals and peers. This has proved to be so popular that other online clubs are quickly being established. Another example is ChemWeb, the worldwide club for the chemical community, which can be found at **http://chemweb.com**.

Do keep in mind the existence of this material provided freely by publishers, since it will be of high quality, current and with a high level of authority. A disadvantage is that you cannot guarantee what information you will find, and it can be a little like going to a car boot or jumble sale, but if you can identify those publishers who produce material that is relevant to your work you can obtain some very useful information from them.

Commercial information

Commercial uses of the Internet could easily take up an entire book in their own right, and I do not intend to go into great detail here; most of what I want to say about commerce and the advanced searcher is covered in Chapter 10. However, it is worth pointing out that publishers are using the Internet to increase revenue, and if you have the budget, you can make use of these services. To illustrate this, I have two examples of companies that are doing a lot of work in this area, and you will be able to see how you can use their systems to obtain information to assist you in your daily work.

My first example is SilverPlatter Information, at **http://www.silverplatter.com**, one of the world's largest CD-ROM publishers, with a total of 90 data owners and 230 different titles. In common with many other publishers, they are now busy repositioning themselves in the market, and they would probably take exception to my description of them as 'CD-ROM publishers', preferring to see themselves as 'electronic publishers'. Most electronic publishers are now ensuring that their customers have greater flexibility in

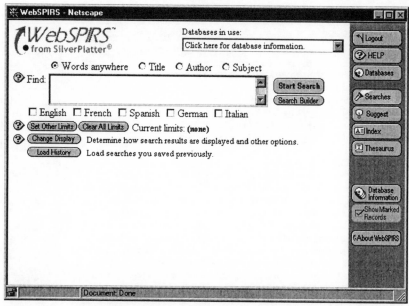

Fig. 6.1 *SilverPlatter WebSPIRS interface*
(WebSPIRS Version 4.01 Copyright 1995–1998 SilverPlatter International NV)

accessing their data; they provide it on optical discs, but the databases can also be copied onto hard disk for faster and as a result of this there is no reason why data in this format cannot be made available to subscribers across the Internet. SilverPlatter has made a version of its search software called WebSPIRS available on the Internet, and I have included a screenshot as Figure 6.1

The interface provides access to all the functionality SilverPlatter customers have come to expect: searching for a word or phrase in the text, title, author and subject searches, access to the database index or thesaurus (if available), and searching by publication year. The reason for this is quite clear – if end-users are familiar with the locally networked or standalone product they will be more likely to search the database across the Internet if the interface looks familiar to them, resulting in a much shallower learning curve. You can run a search, and will be given a results screen similar to that shown in Figure 6.2.

It is at this point that the power of using the Internet as a delivery mechanism for information really comes into its own. Certain elements of the displayed record (such as

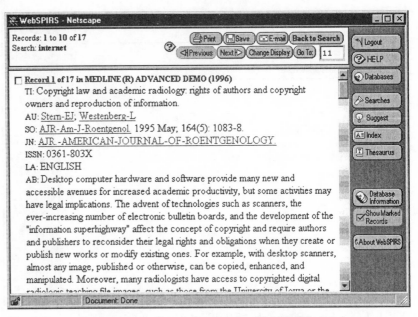

Fig. 6.2   *Partial results from searching a WebSPIRS database*
(WebSPIRS Version 4.01 Copyright 1995–1998 SilverPlatter
International NV)

author or journal, for example) can be highlighted, and those users who are used to Internet conventions will realize that they can click on the highlighted text in order to see all of the articles in the database written by that author, or they can run a search to locate all the articles published in a particular journal. They can of course do the same thing using the traditional version of the software, but the hypertext linking makes the whole process that much more intuitive and straightforward.

The records can then be marked and printed, downloaded or sent via e-mail to a colleague; again the Internet is providing greater flexibility. However, there is more to a Web-based version than this simple level of flexibility, since by the very nature of the medium it becomes much easier to manipulate the data. SilverPlatter has introduced a new product called SilverLinker. This product integrates the full text of journals and bibliographical databases, allowing direct access from the databases to electronic journals available on the Internet. Once an article has been located in a bibliographical search, you may be able to retrieve more information on it by interrogating the library holdings, or order it directly from your preferred document delivery supplier.

The consequences of this approach are clear: it is becoming much easier to dynamically integrate a variety of different systems to link data together for ease of searching and immediate delivery of that data. In the future, the end-user will be able to search for and locate appropriate articles, order the full text of an article and retrieve it via e-mail within a matter of moments, instead of days or weeks. Moreover, the user will be able to do this directly from his/her own desktop, without intervention from the information professional.

It is worth pointing out that WebSPIRS is available for you to try out free of charge. Although the available sample databases are quite small, all of the information is correct, so it may be worthwhile making use of them now and then for a brief overview of a particular subject, or to obtain a few quick references.

Similar work is being done by other electronic publishers, such as Ovid Technologies, based at **http://www.ovid.com**. Ovid aggregates content from their information providers via a single password and server, ensuring that users obtain seamless access to the data they require.

Once again, the implications of this are far-reaching. In the past, because of the nature of the medium, publishers presented data in the form of bound journals. Publishing a single small article of, say, four A4 pages, is not feasible for cost and distribution reasons, but becomes possible when it is included with other articles in a journal. When publishing on the Internet, however, it becomes not only possible, but highly desirable, to make information available in discrete units that can be located and downloaded quickly and easily. As a result, questions can be asked about the future viability of journals in the form that we have known them for the last few hundred years.

The future role of printed journals also becomes less certain when we look at the question of currency. The result of taking an article, printing it and distributing it, is that currency is sacrificed on the altar of distribution. Electronic publication results in articles being published in a matter of minutes instead of weeks or months. Databases can be updated on a daily or hourly basis, instead of taking a month or longer to distribute in optical or paper format. Once again, this raises a

DID YOU KNOW?

If you are wondering how much money is to be made from commercial use of the Internet, the US Commerce Department has estimated that electronic commerce will result in $327 billion business-to-business transactions by the year 2002. Further information on this is available at http://www.forrester.com.

number of questions for the long-term archiving and retrieval of information, which I will address in Chapter 10.

Online journals

I have already mentioned online journals in connection with databases which can be accessed via the Internet, but I think it is important to make a distinction between those and journals which have their own separate 'life' as electronic journals. There are literally thousands of electronic journals which offer high-quality information totally free of charge. These are often in receipt of funding from one organization or another, and exist to promote the free flow of information in their chosen subject area. Two good examples here are *Ariadne* (the Web version is at **http://www.ariadne.ac.uk**) which 'describes and evaluates sources and services available on the Internet and of potential use to librarians and information professionals' and the *Internet resources newsletter* at **http://www.hw.ac.uk/libWWW/irn/irn.html** (please note the capitalization in this URL) which is described as being 'for academics, students, engineers, scientists and social scientists'. Both journals are full of very useful information, and I make sure that I read every single issue. Both are available free of charge, and are very much in the tradition of making information freely available across the Internet.

In many cases, when electronic journals are first established, access to them is free. There are many reasons for this. First, potential readers need to be encouraged to visit the site, and since the publisher cannot give away a binder or free gift as with printed journals, free access can be regarded as a loss leader. Secondly, it is quite difficult to price access to an electronic journal in comparison with a printed version; should it be less, since the publisher does not have the printing and distribution overheads; the same price, since the quality of data should be the same; or indeed should it cost more since readers are getting quicker access to information which can be presented in a wider variety of media? What is swiftly becoming clear to many publishers is that some sort of charge is necessary, since they have to pay writers, designers and programmers, and cover the equipment costs. Some of this money can be recouped by selling advertising space, but it is possible to find only so many advertisers!

Newspapers

Online newspapers, which for the sake of this chapter will be treated like other online journals although there are significant differences, are another splendid source of information for searchers. When I ran a search on Yahoo! for newspapers I came up with 27 categories and 3,579 sites, and I am sure this number will have increased by the time you get to read this. The range of newspapers is quite phenomenal, from regional or city titles such as the *San Francisco Chronicle* at **http://www.sfgate.com** to national newspapers such as the *Electronic Telegraph* at **http://www.telegraph.co.uk**.

Once again, each title is unique and arranges its material as it feels appropriate. Some titles are virtually identical to the paper edition, while others are entirely electronic, and yet others are a combination of these approaches. Some are updated several times during the day, others daily and others again weekly.

However they are updated, and whatever the precise content, online newspapers are one of the very best ways to keep up to date with what is happening within a specific region, city or country, or throughout the world. A sensible searcher will bookmark at least one or two newspapers to refer to regularly.

Bookshops

It is an obvious statement, but bookshops are a wonderful source of information. They do have a number of drawbacks, however, chiefly as a result of being a physical entity! It takes time to go and visit, you need to have a clear idea of what you are looking for, and you need to find the right set of shelves to start hunting through to find appropriate titles. Even when you finally alight on a likely title, you are still not sure it is going to be exactly what you want, so it is then necessary to spend time examining the book before purchasing it. Great fun, of course, but it does use up a frightening amount of time!

Internet bookshops overcome all of these disadvantages, and as a result have become very popular; Yahoo! lists a total of 338 Internet bookshops, 63 based in the UK or Ireland. I'll just explore one in detail to illustrate their value to the information professional.

Amazon.com is one of the largest, if not the largest, bookshops on the Internet, with over 2.5 million titles available, and over 15 million people from 160 countries have purchased titles from their site at **http://www.amazon.com**. Amazon has taken an approach similar to that of BioMedNet, in that they have tried to create a community approach with their data. As well as a straightforward listing of their titles (which of course they have), they have a book-of-the-day section, with an overview of a title and the opportunity to read excerpts, reviews and interviews with the author. Their database can be searched in a number of different ways, by keyword, subject, author, ISBN, publisher, date of publication, and so on.

I ran a search for 'intelligent agents' and was presented with a list of their top three titles and 30 other matches. For most of those I was then able to view the table of contents, obtain a synopsis of the title, read information on the author, and read reviews from people who had already purchased the title. I was also presented with the opportunity to search for titles in related subject areas (one of which was electronic data processing, for example), and Amazon also provides a list of other titles purchased by people who had bought the title I was interested in. Another feature of the site is an automated searcher which informs you when any new titles are published that match criteria that you can set.

Needless to say, you can purchase any of the titles you are interested in (along with a variety of other merchandise such as CDs or T-shirts) by placing them in a 'shopping trolley' which keeps a running total of your expenditure. Once you are satisfied with your selection, your credit card is debited and the titles shipped, usually within a couple of days.

An Internet bookshop such as Amazon is a useful and easy way by which to purchase titles (although I would probably purchase from a bookshop based in the UK to reduce post and packing charges), but is also an excellent way to search for details of books in print. The reviews and guides to similar titles are also an extremely effective method of book selection, and could easily be used by an information professional who had been asked to create a bibliography for an enquirer.

Commercial search engines

As we have seen, most search engines are free for people to use; the organizations that provide them are currently making their money from selling advertising space. Their software is becoming increasingly sophisticated; if you run a search on AltaVista for information on gardens and flowers, you will probably find that you are viewing an advertisement for an Internet florist, for example. While it appears unlikely that the large search engines will charge for standard searches, they may well charge for some of the other services they provide. A good example here is the Northern Light search engine, based at **http://www.northernlight.com/**. Northern Light is a free text search engine, and people who have searched using AltaVista or Lycos will not find it difficult to use. The difference is that Northern Light provides access to what it calls its 'Special Collection sources', which are not available anywhere else on the Internet. Most of these sources go back to January 1995, and some book reviews go back as far as 1990. The collection comprises over 3,400 journals, books, reviews, magazines and newswires.

When searching Northern Light, you have the choice of searching the Web, the special collection or both for no charge. You are able to see abstracts from the special collection for free, but if you wish to view the entire article or document it is necessary to pay a fee. The organization justifies this by explaining that information from the special collection is high-quality, authoritative information which is worth paying for.

Payment is made online via a secure credit-card transaction (prices vary from $1.00 to $4.00), and the document is then displayed on your screen just as though it was another Web page. Northern Light does not offer a subscription service – the system is set up as a 'pay as you go' service.

Summary

Effective searchers will not limit themselves to the major search engines or databases, but instead will keep a very open

DID YOU KNOW?

Entire books are available online which can be read using your browser or downloaded and printed out. This is not only the case for out-of-copyright publications, but also for some books which are still in copyright. A good example is *Digital business*, which is available at **http://www.hammond.co.uk** together with a detailed explanation from the author as to why he has made his title available in this way.

mind about using resources which come from many different sources. In this chapter we have looked at a variety of these, and discussed the ways in which they could be useful. The best information is not always free, and sometimes it is necessary to pay premium prices for premium data, but it is almost always possible to get some worthwhile information out of the free material provided by commercial organizations.

URLs mentioned in this chapter

http://www.smlawpub.co.uk/
http://www.chadwyck.co.uk
http://www.biomednet.com
http://chemweb.com.
http://www.silverplatter.com
http://www.forrester.com
http://www.ovid.com
http://www.ariadne.ac.uk
http://www.hw.ac.uk/libWWW/irn/irn.html
http://www.sfgate.com
http://www.telegraph.co.uk
http://www.amazon.com
http://www.hammond.co.uk
http://www.northernlight.com/

7

Virtual libraries and gateways

Introduction

I have concentrated so far mainly on how to find information
on the Internet by using a variety of different search engines.
This is, of course, an effective way of obtaining information,
but it is not the only way. When, as a user, you go into a
library, you do not expect to have to start searching for information immediately; instead you make use of the signposting
available, or perhaps a map in order to get to the section you
are interested in. Moreover, when you get to the shelves you
expect that the books and other resources will have been
selected by the librarians to cover the subject area and to be
trustworthy sources of information.

This does not automatically happen on the Internet,
unfortunately, since there is no librarian figure who can
check the authority of the data or provide you with all the
appropriate links. However, there do exist virtual libraries
and gateways that can assist in this area. In this chapter I
begin by looking at some of the ways in which you can assess
and evaluate the resources that you discover. Then I go on to
consider the steps that have been taken to provide users with
signposts to valuable information.

Authority on the Internet

This important statement is worth repeating: you cannot
automatically trust the information that you find on the
Web. Since no one is in charge of it, anyone is free to make
available almost any type of information that they wish. I say
'almost', since Web authors are constrained by the laws of the
land. It is not legal for me to libel someone, and making a
libellous statement on a Web site will also leave me open to
prosecution. However, apart from obvious areas such as that,

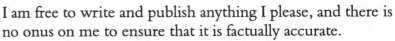

I am free to write and publish anything I please, and there is no onus on me to ensure that it is factually accurate.

It is necessary therefore always to question the information that you find on the Web, and fortunately there are a few helpful ways of checking the authority of a Web site.

The domain name

The first thing that I always check when looking at a Web site is the URL. This tells you a lot about the level of trust you can put in the documents that you find.

You can be assured that if a Web site has **.ac.uk** in the URL it definitely is some sort of British academic site, or if it includes **.gov.uk** it is a British government site. (The situation is different with respect to newsgroups or mailing lists, since even if **.ac.uk** or **.gov.uk** are included in an e-mail address, the individual may well be writing in a personal capacity.) You are slightly less secure with a commercial domain name ending in **.co.uk**, as it is much easier to obtain these. Similarly a **.com** domain name, once used almost exclusively by American commercial organizations, is now widely available, and indeed my own Web site is at **www.philb.com** and I am neither American nor based in the USA; in fact the server which hosts my site is based in Manchester, England. Many internet service providers are now offering free Web space, which is wonderful for budding authors, but simply adds to the confusion for searchers, as the domain name is usually a variant of the ISP's.

In the past it was very easy in many countries to register a domain name, and there were very few checks on who registered what. This has actually led to court cases by high-profile organizations that were not quick enough to register domain names themselves, only to find later that private individuals had already obtained them. In the UK the situation was slightly different, in that laws against 'passing off' already existed, so it was difficult (though not impossible) for individuals to register domain names for well known British companies.

But you should remember that even perfectly legitimate domain names do not necessarily belong to the organizations that you may initially expect.

DID YOU KNOW?

It only costs a few pounds annually to register a domain name, and it is not necessary actually to create a Web site to go with it. Many companies register variants of their names simply to ensure that no one else will be able to use them in the future.

Company logo

The second thing that I check when looking at a Web site is to see if it carries a recognizable company or organizational logo. This is not a foolproof method of ensuring the legitimacy of the site, of course, but it does provide further corroborating evidence. Copyright laws exist on the Internet in the same way that they exist elsewhere, and individuals cannot simply copy any material that they find on Web sites; if they do, they run the risk of receiving a sharp solicitor's letter telling them to cease and desist! Many companies are very strict in the use that can be made of their logos, sometimes to the extent of refusing to allow them to be used as a graphic link from other sites back to their own.

Contact details

Every site on the Web has been created by someone at some time. I am much more likely to treat a Web site seriously if it provides contact details for the author or person responsible for the site. Then I know that if I have problems, either technically or with the information on the site, there is someone I can contact about them. If no contact details are given (and this happens surprisingly often), it makes me wonder what is wrong with the site, since no one is prepared to take responsibility for the data on it.

Currency

When I view a Web site, I want to make sure that the data on it is current. It is of usually easy to check this with a printed publication, but almost impossible to do so with a Web site, unless the author gives details of when the site was last updated. If no date is given I have no way of easily checking this and am much less inclined to take the information found on the site seriously. A good Web site is constantly being updated, and I would expect to find something new, altered or updated at least monthly. Any longer than this can imply that the organization is not taking the site seriously, which casts doubt on the validity of the data. (I am of course referring to data that would be expected to change regularly.)

DID YOU KNOW?

You will often see discussions centred on the fact that domain names are going to run out. What is actually meant is that good domain names will run out. The potential number of different domain names that are available is:

1,075,911,801,979,990,000,00 0,000,000,000,000,000,000,00 0,000,000,000,000,000,000

DID YOU KNOW?

Copyright laws apply to the Internet in the same way that they do to printed matter. If you don't have permission from the copyright holder to use an image or text, you are probably breaking the law.

Awards

I quite often see sites boasting of the awards which they have won, usually accompanied by a garish medal of some description. In my opinion, these are not worth the paper they are (not) printed on. Since there are no official Internet bodies, any awards are offered by individuals or companies, and it is often quite difficult to find out exactly what the criteria are for winning an award. As a result, I retain a healthy scepticism about them.

Page design

In many cases, Web page design is entirely down to an individual's personal choice, and simply because the page is displayed as red text on a green background does not automatically invalidate the information it contains. However, if an individual or organization cares about their site they should ensure that the pages can be viewed well using any browser in any screen resolution. Anything less implies once again that they are not taking their site seriously, so I am less inclined to trust the data that I find.

As I have demonstrated, there are many things that need to be taken into account when assessing the authority of a site, but the experienced searcher will quickly become adept at sorting out the wheat from the chaff. However, if you are working in an unfamiliar area, it does become more difficult, and this is where virtual libraries can play an important role.

Checking against other sources

It almost goes without saying that it is worthwhile checking the information that you retrieve off a Web page with a known source of good data. It would of course be possible to check every single fact you find on one site against those you find on another, but that way lies madness. If you have to be certain about the authority of the information you are going to be using, simply choose one fact which can be quickly and easily checked against another source. If the results tally, then you can be reasonably reassured that other data on the site is accurate, and if they do not, then you may need to do a little more research to be certain that you can reliably use the information.

What is a virtual library?

Virtual libraries are called many different things: gateways, digital collections, digital libraries and cyber libraries are just a few of the terms in current use. Whatever they are called, they have certain things in common.

- They are collaborative ventures in which information professionals and other experts in specific subject areas pool their knowledge and experience to collate information on a specific subject.
- Information is checked for accuracy and authority.
- Their geographical position is not important – the focus is on the information contained within them rather than on which continent they are located.
- Data is displayed clearly and concisely, allowing for easy navigation.
- They are kept current.

What does a virtual library contain?

Since all virtual libraries are slightly different, it is not possible to give a complete listing of everything that you might find in one – you'll have to discover that for yourself! However, you can generally expect to find a mixture of the following:

- links to other Web sites and resources
- newsletters, either about the subject area or about the virtual library itself
- databases of resources listed at the library, and links to databases which cover the particular subject area
- subject guides to provide you with more information and background in the various specialisms covered by the subject area
- documents (full text)
- lists of meetings, conferences and exhibitions
- information about mailing lists and newsgroups in the subject area
- what's new and information announcements
- bibliographies
- books in electronic format

■ reports and papers.

When should an information professional use a virtual library?

There are almost as many reasons why you should consider using a virtual library as there are libraries! Some of the major reasons are:

■ Virtual libraries provide authoritative, factual information
■ If time is short, they are a useful resource since they contain focused, appropriate information. Search engines, while useful, will often return large numbers of hits, even with very precise searches, and many of these may have limited relevance to the subject.
■ Virtual libraries generally provide precise, accurate descriptions of information, saving time when trying to decide which resource to look at.
■ Virtual libraries are kept current, so there should be few, if any, broken links.
■ Virtual libraries collect subject-specific materials in one place.
■ They provide an overview of a subject, which is useful if you have limited knowledge of that subject.

Virtual libraries currently available
The WWW Virtual Library

The WWW Virtual Library is the oldest catalogue of the Web. It was begun by Tim Berners-Lee, the 'founding father' of the Web, and is in fact a collection of subject-specific libraries, a list of which is available at **http://vlib.stanford. edu/Overview.html**. It runs from aboriginal studies to zoos, with beer and brewing, civil engineering, philosophy and waste-water engineering in between. The libraries associated with the WWW Virtual Library generally display a particular logo which, although it is in the public domain and therefore can be used by anyone, has become associated with them. This is shown in Figure 7.1. Figure 7.2 shows the Virtual Library home page at Stanford, and there is also a mirror site in the UK at **http://www.mth.uea.ac.uk/**

Fig. 7.1   *The WWW Virtual Library logo*

VL/Overview.html. However, the main URL for the WWW Virtual Library is **http://www.w3.org/vl/** as the others are subject to change at short notice.

The WWW Virtual Library does not exist in one single place, but is distributed around the world, individual libraries being held on different servers, maintained by different people. At present it does not have a formal structure, but an ad hoc committee is currently looking at creating one. Consequently, the information that you will find in each of the component virtual libraries differs in accordance with the subject under consideration.

The eLib Programme

eLib, the Electronic Libraries Programme at **http://www. ukoln.ac.uk/services/elib/** in conjunction with JISC at **http://www.jisc.ac.uk** has been instrumental in the establishment of a number of virtual libraries, in particular a project called ROADS (Resource Organisation And Discovery in Subject-based Services), which is a confederation of virtual

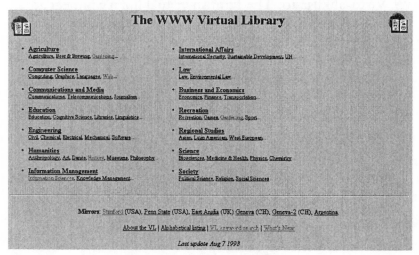

Fig. 7.2   *The WWW Virtual Library home page*

libraries, based in the UK.

ROADS performs a number of different operations; it has produced software to enable the creation of virtual libraries, investigates methods of cross-searching between gateways, and assists in the development of indexing, cataloguing and searching resources.

There are a number of different subject-specific gateways within the ROADS system; for an overview you can visit their site at **http://www.ilrt.bris.ac.uk/roads/who/**, or you may prefer just to jump in and go directly to look at some of the sites themselves. The following is a list of current gateways which are associated with the eLib project, but more are being added all the time.

- ADAM: Art, Design, Architecture and Media at **http://www.adam.ac.uk**
- ALEX: a catalogue of electronic texts at **http://sunsite.berkeley.edu/~emorgan/alex**
- Biz/ed: Business and economics at **http://www.bized.ac.uk**
- The Countryside Recreation Network at **http://www.ilrt.bris.ac.uk/crn/**
- EELS: Engineering Electronic Library, Sweden at **http://www.ub2.lu.se/eel/eelhome.html**
- EEVL: The Edinburgh Engineering Virtual Library at **http://www.eevl.ac.uk**
- Virtuaalikirjasto: The Finnish virtual library project at **http://www.uku.fi/kirjasto/virtuaalikirjasto/**
- HISTORY: **http://ihr.sas.ac.uk**
- NETEG: Netskills Network Education and Training Electronic Gateway at **http://www.netskills.ac.uk/NETEG/**
- OMNI: Organising Medical Networked Information at **http://www.omni.ac.uk**
- OWL: Orthopaedic Web Links at **http://osl.os.qub.ac.uk**
- RUDI: Resource for Urban Design Information at **http://rudi.herts.ac.uk**
- SOSIG: Social Science Information Gateway at **http://www.sosig.ac.uk/**

■ WWEVL: Waste Water Engineering Virtual Library at **http://www.cleanh2o.com/cleanh2o/ww/ welcome.html**.

The ROADS gateways differ in a number of significant respects from the WWW Virtual Library:

■ The sites are not static, in that they offer searchable databases of manually catalogued resources. Most of the WWW Virtual Libraries have to be searched page by page to discover the information required.
■ The subject coverage is not as wide as the WWW Virtual Libraries, although those subjects which are covered tend to be in more depth, often with over three thousand resources being catalogued.
■ ROADS sites tend to run computerized procedures to automatically check that links are still active, and they periodically check the resources to ensure that the descriptions given are still accurate.

Other virtual libraries

Of course, not all virtual libraries are involved in the ROADS system, and a good example of an independent library (which also receives no funding) is HUMBUL, the HUManities BULletin Board at **http://users.ox.ac.uk/ ~humbul**. As the name suggests, HUMBUL concentrates on the humanities, and covers subjects such as anthropology, archaeology, the classics, dictionaries, history, language and linguistics, libraries, music and, religious studies, to name but a few.

A comprehensive list of some 44 virtual libraries and gateways can be found at **http://www.scran.ac.uk/cgi-bin/ links/view.pl** by clicking on 'Other Subject Gateways'.

A virtual library in action

Having looked at virtual libraries in general terms, let us now look at one in action. I've chosen to look at BUBL, based at **http://www.bubl.ac.uk** which is a JISC-funded information service designed for the UK higher-education community. However, its use is much wider than that, since it is

DID YOU KNOW?

When the service began in 1990, BUBL stood for BUlletin Board for Libraries, but it is now generally referred to as the BUBL Information Service.

BUBL Information Service

HOME LINK JOURNALS SEARCH NEWS UK MAIL ARCHIVE ADMIN

A national information service for the higher education community, funded by JISC

BUBL Link
Catalogue of selected Internet resources

BUBL Search
Search BUBL or beyond

BUBL UK
The UK home page

BUBL Archive
LIS, journals, Internet development

BUBL Journals
Abstracts, full text, hundreds of titles

BUBL News
Jobs, events, surveys, updates

BUBL Mail
Mailing lists and mail archives

BUBL Admin
About BUBL: FAQ, feedback, funding ...

BUBL Information Service, Andersonian Library, Strathclyde University, 101 St James Road, Glasgow G4 0NS, Scotland
Tel: 0141 548 4752   *Email*: bubl@bubl.ac.uk

Fig. 7.3   *The BUBL Information Service home page*

used by academic communities in the UK and abroad, as well as by librarians, information professionals, and indeed anyone with access to the Internet. The major aim of the service is to 'provide clear, fast and reliable access to selected information sources, which means no adverts, no animations, and few graphics.' The home page is reproduced as Figure 7.3; as can be seen, it provides access to a very wide variety of information, though its particular strength is in UK-oriented material. From BUBL UK it is possible quickly to find information on aspects of the UK such as central government, political parties, newspapers, the media, UK Web directories, academic information, hospitals, libraries, museums and so on.

BUBL LINK is a database or catalogue of Internet resources of academic relevance, with each resource being evaluated, classified and catalogued before being added. It is organized by the Dewey Decimal Classification system, and can be browsed by subject or class number. The section on library and information services is arranged as follows:

020   Library and information science: general resources
020   Library and information science: departments
020   Library and information science: discussion lists
020   Library and information science: journals
020.6 Library organisations
021   Co-operation and resource sharing

023   Personnel administration
025   Operations of libraries and information centres
027.4 Public libraries
027.5 National and government libraries
027.7 University and college libraries
027.8 School libraries

Specific searches can be undertaken using the BUBL Search
interface. The major differences between doing a search in
BUBL rather than using a general search engine are as follows:

- A smaller, focused set of resources is used, reducing the
  number of results returned, and thereby saving time.
- The user obtains more information about the site, such as
  resource type (bibliography, index, documents, articles).
- The name of the author or organization responsible for
  each site found is immediately available.

I ran a search for 'Intelligent agents' on BUBL LINK, and
reproduced the results in Figure 7.4. As can be seen, this
resulted in a total number of 7 hits (including those listed
under the entry 006.3 Intelligent software agents). The same
search run on AltaVista resulted in 1,910,702 possible
matches. This is perhaps not a fair comparison, since I would
normally have been much more specific in an AltaVista
search, but even a very precise search would have resulted in
far too many hits, and it would have been necessary to visit
each site in turn to check and see if it contained the type of
information I wanted. Using the BUBL service I can rest
assured that the sites found are going to be of high quality
and will be appropriate to me as an information professional.
   BUBL has also recently introduced a new service, entitled
5:15, which is a different interface to the LINK database.
This allows you to select from over 1,100 predetermined
search terms without having to type anything. This will
return at least five and usually no more than 15 items for
each subject. An abstract and catalogue record is made available for each item, all the links have been checked within the
last month, and over 50% of the items are resources found in

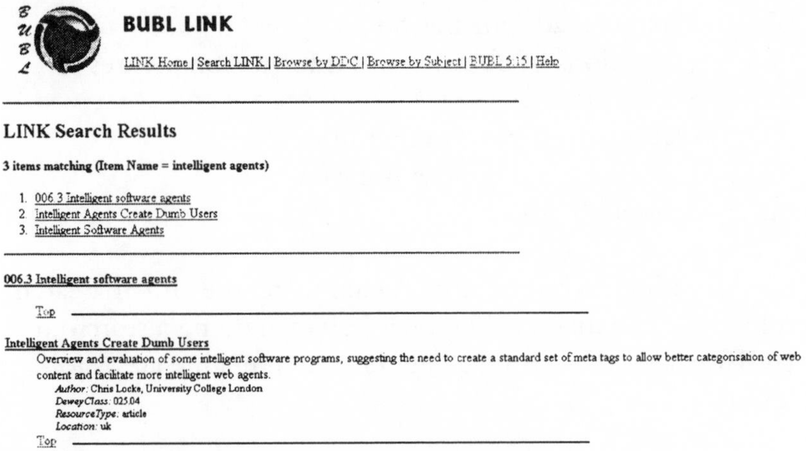

BUBL LINK

LINK Home | Search LINK | Browse by DDC | Browse by Subject | BUBL 5.15 | Help

LINK Search Results

3 items matching (Item Name = intelligent agents)

1. 006.3 Intelligent software agents
2. Intelligent Agents Create Dumb Users
3. Intelligent Software Agents

006.3 Intelligent software agents

Top

Intelligent Agents Create Dumb Users

Overview and evaluation of some intelligent software programs, suggesting the need to create a standard set of meta tags to allow better categorisation of web content and facilitate more intelligent web agents.
Author: Chris Locke, University College London
DeweyClass: 025.04
ResourceType: article
Location: uk

Top

Fig. 7.4   *Results of a search at BUBL LINK*

the UK or elsewhere outside the USA.

BUBL also provides a journal service that contains over 140 LIS journals, magazines and newsletters. Several of these are the full text, while others contain just contents and abstracts, and some are contents only. This ensures you can keep up to date with developments in the industry quickly and effectively.

Summary

Virtual libraries and gateways are an extremely useful way of ensuring that you can limit the results of a search to a manageable number of hits that are current, informative and authoritative. Their strength lies in the fact that the resources made available have been evaluated and selected, and in the summaries, which are created by professionals who work in the area in which the library operates. Paradoxically, however, this is also their weakness, since this human intervention takes time and a lot of voluntary effort, which may mean that the resources listed are not as current as they should be. Nonetheless, a virtual library is always a good way to begin exploring a subject area, safe in the knowledge that the information retrieved will always be of high quality.

URLs mentioned in this chapter

http://www.philb.com

http://vlib.stanford.edu/Overview.html
http://www.w3.org/vl/
http://www.mth.uea.ac.uk/VL/Overview.html
http://www.ukoln.ac.uk/services/elib/
http://www.jisc.ac.uk
http://www.ilrt.bris.ac.uk/roads/who/
http://www.adam.ac.uk
http://sunsite.berkeley.edu/~emorgan/alex
http://www.bized.ac.uk
http://www.ilrt.bris.ac.uk/crn/
http://www.ub2.lu.se/eel/eelhome.html
http://www.eevl.ac.uk
http://www.uku.fi/kirjasto/virtuaalikirjasto/
http://ihr.sas.ac.uk
http://www.netskills.ac.uk/NETEG/
http://www.omni.ac.uk
http://osl.os.qub.ac.uk
http://rudi.herts.ac.uk
http://www.sosig.ac.uk/
http://www.cleanh2o.com/cleanh2o/ww/
    welcome.html
http://users.ox.ac.uk/~humbul
http://www.scran.ac.uk/cgi-bin/links/view.pl
http://www.bubl.ac.uk

Part 2

Becoming an expert searcher

8

Intelligent agents

Introduction
In this chapter we'll look at intelligent agents in some detail. As you will see, intelligent agents are the next logical extension of search engines, in that they do a lot of the work of searching for you. There are a number of different types, some commercial, some free. I will focus on the ways in which they can be used, giving examples of some of the best known.

What is an intelligent agent?
The problem with all of the search engines that we have looked at so far is the necessity to go back to them regularly to update the results that you've found. As we've already seen, it is possible to do this by bookmarking the search page, going back to it, and re-running the search. With a search engine like AltaVista you can put in a new date limiter to retrieve just the most recent results. However, this is a rather laborious approach, and one that can take up a lot of time. Furthermore, you then have to visit each site in turn to see if it is actually of any use to you.

This is where the concept of intelligent agents comes into play. Imagine a situation where you are an end-user seeking information; you go into a library and ask the librarian for some information about your chosen subject. The librarian goes away and finds information that may or may not be exactly what you are looking for, so you keep some material and discard the rest. The librarian takes a note of what you keep and what you decide not to use, and goes away again, to return a few minutes later with more information which more closely matches your enquiry. The librarian has learned, from looking at what you find useful and what you

HINTS AND TIPS
If you have to provide a current awareness service, consider using an intelligent agent; this will save you a lot of time as you will not need to keep re-running searches – the intelligent agent will do that for you.

don't, the exact type of material you're interested in, and this results in the retrieval of new, more appropriate information. This is of course very helpful, but our librarian is even more efficient than that, because the next time you go into the library you find a pile of new books and magazines waiting for you, with the latest up-to-date information on your subject.

Advantages and disadvantages of intelligent agents

Essentially, an intelligent agent is a piece of software that learns from your responses, and is able to search the Web while you are not there, looking for more information which can then be presented to you when you log on next time. The advantages of this approach are easy to see – you get good-quality information covering your subject, it is current and you don't need to go looking for it yourself, therefore saving you time.

The disadvantages are, however, equally obvious. In order for the intelligent agent to understand what you are interested in and to focus its search more closely, you have to spend quite a long time with it initially; 'training' it to find the good material and ignore the bad. Equally, you are reliant on the agent to look in the right places. You might be able to find some useful information for yourself by searching the Web, but if the agent doesn't know about a particular source it is not going to be able to use it when looking for appropriate data. Consequently, there will almost always be a degree of uncertainty as to whether you've got all the information that is available to you.

A further problem is that an intelligent agent is of little use if you want to do a 'quick and dirty' search to start you off. In the time that it might take to train an agent, you could have run a search, found some information in the right area which matches your query, passed the data onto your user and be considering where to go for lunch! Computers are wonderful at number crunching, but they fail miserably when you need an intuitive approach. However, if you are running a current awareness service an intelligent agent may well be the best approach to take. It will present you with a variety of results, and you can then just pick the best, saving you the time and energy it would otherwise have taken to run the search once a month, or even once a day.

Intelligent agents on the Web

Having discussed some of the background issues, let's now take a closer look at how these intelligent agents have been implemented on the Web, and the ways in which you can make use of them. As you would expect, there are a variety of different approaches, and I'll take them one at a time. We'll start by taking a look at one or two implementations which don't have much use in the day-to-day work of the information professional, but which will give you a clearer idea of how these things work. Besides, they are quite amusing!

Intelligent agents that shop for you

I'm sure you've been faced with a situation where you're looking for a present for someone, or indeed a treat for yourself, but you don't know quite what you want. This certainly happens to me – I'll go into a record store or a video shop and look at an item, then put it back down again because I'm not prepared to spend the money on a product without knowing whether I'll like it or not. Thanks to intelligent agents, I can now choose products that I know I will like.

First of all, you'll need to visit the home of an intelligent agent, and the example that I'll use here is one called 'Firefly' which can be found at **http://www.firefly.net/**. You need to obtain a 'passport' to use their system, which basically just means choosing a name and password, and providing some basic information such as e-mail address and date of birth. This then allows you to search a number of different sites, and to personalize them according to your own specific choices and tastes. One of these, for example, is **http://www.filmfinder.com/**; this allows you to choose movies that you have seen and rate them on a scale. After you have done about 20 of these you can ask the system to make recommendations based on the responses you have given, and these are sometimes uncannily accurate. If films are not your idea of a good time, there are other sites that

DID YOU KNOW?

The original intelligent agent or 'bot' is ELIZA, written in 240 lines of code, which is supposed to simulate a psychotherapist.

ELIZA is classed as a 'ChatterBot' since she talks back to you. A more recent version, Shallow Red, is rather more sophisticated. You can discover more about both of them by visiting **http://www.chatter-bots.com**.

will do the same sort of thing, only with books or music.

At the moment such things are chiefly of novelty value, but their potential is much greater than that. If you have a few minutes to spare (as well as some money!) you may wish to visit other intelligent agents at **http://www. shoppingexplore.com** and try them out for yourself.

Having seen how these agents work in the area of shopping and choosing products, I'm sure you can appreciate how intelligent agents can be put to good use in the area of information gathering. They can present you with news and current events information, or can search out Web pages that you may be interested in viewing. This brings us to the next type of intelligent agent, which I've called the intelligent newspaper.

Intelligent newspapers

Perhaps the easiest way to see how intelligent agents work is to look at some of the personalized newspapers that are currently available on the Web. These are beginning to appear quite regularly now, and are an extremely good way of keeping up to date in subject areas that are of interest to you. As you might expect, some are more intelligent than others. The majority of these newspapers allow you to define broad areas of interest, such as world news, politics, weather, business briefings and so on. Some also allow you to list a historical fact of the day, your horoscope, or even your favourite cartoon strip!

Each time you visit your intelligent newspaper it will update for you, providing you with the latest news in the subject categories that you have chosen. Consequently, the newspaper will ensure that you get to see new breaking stories, latest stocks and shares information, and so on. In order to do this, the newspaper will visit a variety of different sources on your behalf – Web sites, news sources and so on – and will either display these on the screen in their entirety, or give you the headline, with a link to the source, allowing you to click on the link to read the story.

CRAYON

A good example of a personalized newspaper can be found at

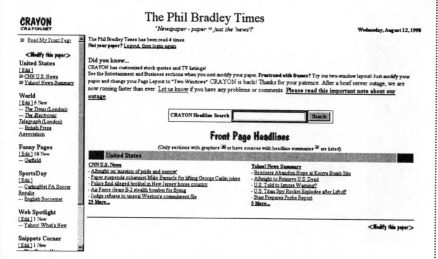

Fig. 8.1   *'The Phil Bradley Times' at CRAYON*
(Copyright 1998 NetPressence, Inc.)

http://www.crayon.net (CReAte Your Own Newspaper).
Figure 8.1 shows you a recent copy of 'The Phil Bradley
Times'.

This personalized newspaper took about five minutes to
create, simply by choosing the subject areas that I was interested in from a large list of general and specific subject areas.
I then had to decide on the way in which I wanted the paper
to be laid out on the screen (as you can see, I created it as a
frames page, with summary information on the left, and the
main body of the text in the right-hand frame). I then bookmarked the page, so that when I return to it in the future it
will recognize who I am and dynamically refresh the page,
updating the information contained within it.

Autonomy Knowledge Update

Another product, similar to CRAYON, is the Autonomy
Knowledge Update. It is produced by Autonomy
(**http://www.agentware.com**), and allows you to keep
agents working on your behalf, which can be trained on any
subjects that you have an interest in. Figure 8.2 illustrates my
personalized news page, with an agent called CD-ROM,
which I've trained to find me appropriate information for my
particular interests in that subject area.

The agent(s) will then search more than 50 online newspa-

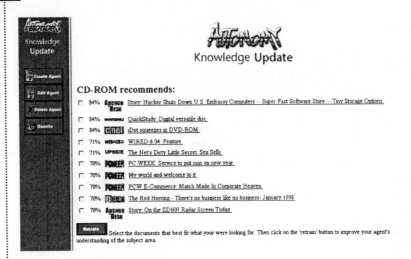

Fig. 8.2   *An Autonomy Knowledge Update list of suggested news stories relating to CD-ROM*

pers for you, basically creating your own daily newspaper. This 'newspaper' can be automatically updated whenever you log into the site, and you can compile a new section when you wish, simply by editing, creating or deleting an agent.

In some respects it is slightly more intelligent than CRAYON, since it will modify the news that it presents to you in response to the headlines that you have previously looked at. It gives you the opportunity of 'retraining' your agent, which is where it becomes of rather more value than CRAYON. You can click on an article that interests you to view it, then check the box next to that article, which gives your agent a clearer idea of what exactly interests you. The agent looks at the article you liked, and identifies key ideas and concepts that it contains. It is then able to use this information to create a profile that matches your interests even more closely. Figure 8.3 shows a selection of the news items that the Autonomy Knowledge Update found for me in the same subject area once I had retrained it by marking those stories which I found particularly appropriate.

Most of these newspapers tend to be heavily oriented towards the USA, but this is not too much of a problem if you are interested in information from around the world. Both CRAYON and the Autonomy Knowledge Update give you considerable freedom in customizing your newspaper,

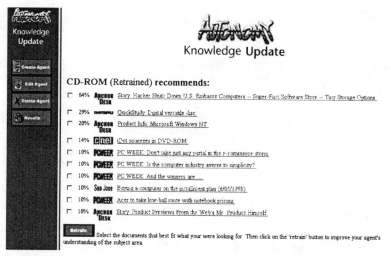

Fig. 8.3   *The Autonomy Knowledge Update CD-ROM agent retrained to provide more focused results*

allowing you to rearrange the order and priority of the information that is presented to you. Moreover, both will search a number of international newspapers if you wish, and will display headlines from the Electronic Telegraph or other British newspapers. There are only a very few subject areas that are specific to the USA, such as television listings. CRAYON also gives American users an opportunity to input their zip code, and can then provide them with local information. I expect that future enhancements of intelligent newspapers will extend their coverage by allowing greater customization for users from other countries. In the meantime, remember that you probably want to choose Soccer, rather than Football, when setting up a page! UK-based newspapers are beginning to offer similar features; *The Times* had an option for personalizing your copy of the newspaper, though at the time of writing this has been withdrawn pending upgrades and improvement.

Intelligent search engines

Search engines are constantly looking for ways in which to increase their user base, and as a result the concept of intelligent agents is very appealing. Search engines have large databases available to them, so the inclusion of an intelligent agent is a natural next step. The search engine can interrogate

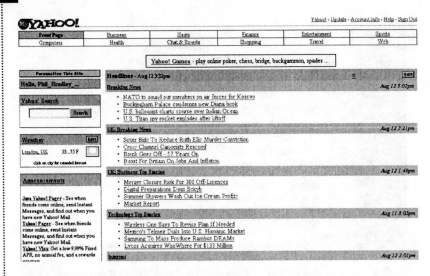

Fig. 8.4   *'My Yahoo!' front page designed according to my own preferences*

a user request and then provide either an updating service or suggestions as to other potentially useful sites.

'My Yahoo!'

'My Yahoo!' is one of the stable of products produced by the Yahoo! Corporation. It allows you to create your own user profile, based on the Yahoo! system of subject headings and current events. The basics of the system are quite simple: you visit Yahoo! at **http://www.yahoo.com**, input details on yourself (name, password and so on), and choose from a number of broad categories (such as business, entertainment or a stock portfolio) and subdivisions beneath those. These then form the basis of your personalized page.

Yahoo! is able to create a user profile based on this information. It can then create pages on the fly specifically for you, and display news and current events information covering your areas of interest. If you have an interest in baseball, want to know what the weather is like in Florida, and you also want to check the winning numbers in the California lottery, 'My Yahoo!' can instantly do this for you. If you also need to be kept informed about stock prices and the latest corporate takeover in the telecommunications world, a simple mouse click to take you to the Business section of your pages keeps you instantly up to speed.

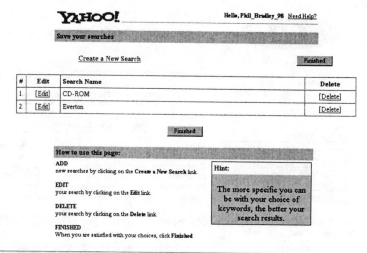

Fig. 8.5 *Personalized news topics in 'My Yahoo!'*

Figure 8.4 shows the front page that 'My Yahoo!' has created for me, listing a variety of news headlines, both from around the world and in specific subject areas. At the top of the page you can see a number of different subject headings, such as 'Web', 'Business' and 'Entertainment'. If I click on any of these, Yahoo! will then display new information in these areas.

'My Yahoo!' also allows you to store frequently run Yahoo! searches, and offers a 'News Clipping' service, which enables you to create your own searches which you can store and run whenever you wish, to keep you fully up to date with what is happening in your area(s) of interest. Figure 8.5 indicates part of the process of setting up personalized searches. You can specify the name of the search, and there is an edit feature that allows you to add or change the search terms that are being used. Once you have created the searches required, a click on the 'Finished' button sends the details back to your personalized page, and the searches can then be run whenever required.

'My Yahoo!' does not bring information directly to your desktop, since you have to visit the site in order to obtain the new information, but you can always bookmark the page and tell Yahoo! how often you want it to be updated, so it is the next best thing. If you use the same computer to connect to

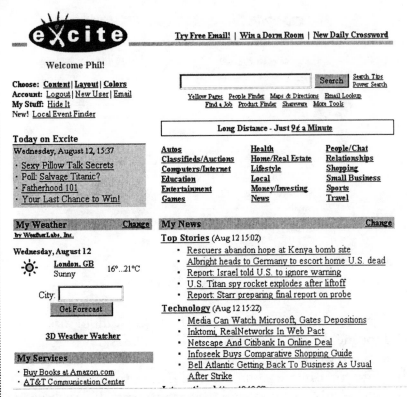

Fig. 8.6   *A personalized Excite Web page*

'My Yahoo!' it is intelligent enough to work out who you are and immediately display an updated version of your pages without you having to do any more work. However, if you log onto the system from another computer you will need to login with your user name and password before accessing your pages. Remember that you should also log out at the end of the session, or 'My Yahoo!' will allow anyone who uses the computer afterwards to log into your pages and change the parameters that you have established!

Other search engine intelligent agents

If you do not like the way in which Yahoo! has implemented their intelligent agent facility, I would suggest looking at some of the other search engines. Many of them have realized that in order to be competitive they have to offer the same features and functionality, and over the next few months I predict that all search engines will allow users to personalize them. Figure 8.6 shows how Excite has implemented 'Phil's Channel'. You can create your own version at **http://www.excite.com**, or you could visit Lycos at **http://www.personal.lycos.com** or HotBot at **http://www.wired.com/newbot/personal_agent.html**.

Intelligent utilities

By now you can see how useful intelligent agents can be when you are producing profiles for individuals or departments. Consequently this is a growth area, and an increasing number of organizations are offering software utilities which exploit this opportunity. In this section I give some examples of companies which are doing just that.

PointCast

The PointCast Network (PCN) at **http://www.pointcast. com** uses 'push technology' to send personalized information directly to your desktop. Although this is not an intelligent agent in the sense that it learns from your interests and modifies the data that it sends to you, it enables you to choose data from a wide variety of subject areas which is then 'pushed' through to you. Unlike many other services, the PointCast utility sits happily in the background, sending information through to you automatically, or at the specific times you have requested. It is, therefore, a constantly updating source of information in the areas of general/political/international news, weather, lifestyle, health, regional data, stocks, sport and so on. It can even provide you with a daily horoscope! PCN takes newsfeeds from regional and international sources, but it has a very definite bias towards the USA, although there are regional variations for Canada and the Far East. However, I expect the service to expand in the future to encompass other regions of the world, and consequently it is worth keeping an eye on. PCN works with both the major browsers, and allows you to move quickly from headlines to Web pages and so on. Figure 8.7 illustrates a page of data retrieved by PCN.

A variety of specialist PointCasts have been developed, such as the College Network Edition (information from over 120 American campuses), Government Insider Edition,

DID YOU KNOW?

Most of the time you spend on the Web you are pulling information down from servers around the world onto your computer. At your command your browser connects to the remote server hosting the page and copies the data back onto your hard disk to display for you. This obviously requires work on your part, and the page remains static, in that the browser obtained the copy of the page that was available at the time. 'Push' technology works slightly differently, in that the remote server takes responsibility for updating the page and pushing it through to you on a regular basis without your having to refresh the page for yourself.

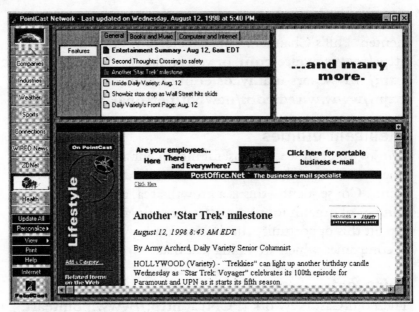

Fig. 8.7   *A PointCast Network update page*

HealthCare Insider Edition, and so on. PCN plans to increase the number of these specialized editions, generating higher revenue streams via advertising.

WebCompass

WebCompass has been produced by Quarterdeck Corporation, and they describe it as a '"search brain" that finds, ranks and analyses the information you really want, then presents it so you can understand it.' Detailed information on the product and the company can be found at **http://www.qdeck.com**, and you can also download the utility from this site.

WebCompass works by using a variety of search engines (35 engines at the moment, although you can specify others if you wish) simultaneously on your behalf. It collates the results and visits each site in turn, choosing appropriate keywords, and builds summaries of each of the sites, and ranks these findings in relevance order. You can then browse through the results and visit the pages of interest.

However, the software allows you to do more than this, since you can focus in on particular keywords and get WebCompass to check for new information. It can perform

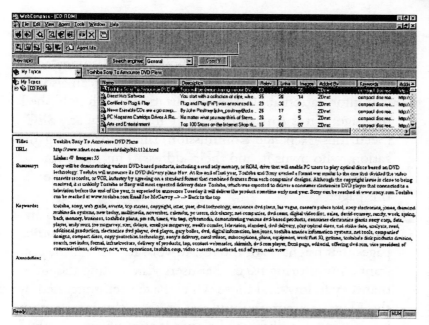

Fig. 8.8 *WebCompass in action*

regular automatic updates while you are connected to the Internet, but if it is not practical to have a constant connection you can configure WebCompass to update whenever you log on. You'll notice here that I've said 'the Internet', rather than the Web, since the product will also search newsgroups, FTP and gopher sites. Figure 8.8 shows WebCompass working; in this instance it has looked for, and is displaying, information on CD-ROM technology, using keywords that it has suggested and also ones that I have specified.

Alexa

Alexa is another intelligent agent, located at **http://www.alexa.com**, but this one works slightly differently from those we have already looked at. When you run a search, it sits in the background and communicates with the browser to call up site statistics and related links from its vast database of information. It is then able to provide you with useful information that is otherwise difficult to obtain. Examples of the data it provides are:

■ Information on where you are. The Alexa client ensures that you are better informed about the page and site being viewed, such as how large it is, how often it is updated, how fast it loads and how popular it is. Alexa can also give you information about the organization which published the page; if it is American it will tell you about any SEC (Securities Exchange Commission) filings for the organization, who owns it, and their address. This helps you answer the question 'Can I trust the data that I find on this page?'

■ Links you can follow. Alexa checks the page that you are viewing, refers back to its own servers and suggests other pages that might be of interest to you. It does this by constantly monitoring pages that users visit, noting the links that they follow, and those which have been suggested by the Alexa user community, and presents this information to you via its toolbar (see below). It also achieves this by looking at words and phrases on the Web page and finding other pages that contain the same information.

■ A Web archive. Alexa has archived over 10 terabytes of Web page data from over 900,000 Web sites, and takes a new 'snapshot' of the Web every 30–60 days. If you are trying to visit a page which no longer exists, or which is blocking access, it is possible to use the Alexa archive to retrieve a copy of the page if it has been visited by the Alexa robot. As a result, you may be able to see data which otherwise would not have been available to you, but of course you must remember that this data is not current, which calls into question its reliability.

All this is achieved through the use of a small toolbar, which floats unobtrusively on top of the browser and can be accessed immediately. Figure 8.9 shows you an example of what this toolbar looks like.

The toolbar tells you which page you are on (in this case Alexa Internet), and how popular it is (in the top 10,000 of

DID YOU KNOW?

The Alexa database is over 10 terabytes in size. One terabyte is a million megabytes or 1,099,511,627,776 bytes in size. In other words – an awful lot of information!.

Fig. 8.9   The Alexa toolbar

visited pages), and if you click on the triangle icon Alexa provides more information about the page and the company which produced it. The next section displays a list of links which Alexa thinks will be the ones most useful to you, and the small 'temple' icon will retrieve the selected page from Alexa's archive if the browser cannot immediately retrieve it. The final icon takes you directly into a number of useful reference resources, such as Encyclopaedia Britannica, the Merriam-Webster Online Dictionary and Thesaurus, and the Britannica Internet Guide, which includes reviews and ratings of over 90,000 Web sites.

The strength (and indeed the difference) of this utility is that it learns from its user community, rather than solely relying on a series of algorithms. By keeping track of what people are looking at, and where they are going, Alexa can predict what other pages users will be interested in, in a way which is not possible when using the other intelligent agents mentioned in this chapter. The only disadvantage of the utility is that it will not be able to provide you with a great deal of information if you are searching a subject area that other Alexa users have not previously explored, in which case its ability to predict other useful sites is limited. In such cases Alexa defaults to the use of link and text analysis to derive related sites until enough users have encountered the site through their Web travels. I think that perhaps its strongest point is its ability to confirm the authority of a site quickly and easily with a simple mouse click, presenting you with information that would otherwise take a lot of extra search time to uncover.

Commercial intelligent agents

We have now seen a number of different types of intelligent agents and how they work. There are many more agents that I have not talked about so far, mainly because they are primarily designed for commercial purposes, rather than searching the Internet. It is not difficult to imagine the ways in which such agents work. An intelligent agent used by a supermarket will be able to track your purchases on a regular basis, and will be able to remind you that it is time to put in an order for cat litter, for example! It will also be able to alert you to new products that it thinks you would like, or bring information about special offers to your attention.

An intelligent agent used by an Internet bookshop will also learn about the kind of books that you are interested in reading and will be able to alert you via e-mail (to give one example) of any new publications in an area which interests you, or which are by your favourite author.

Database providers can use intelligent agents to follow your search profiles, run searches on your behalf whenever the database is updated and e-mail the results to you. Indeed, there is no reason why they should not be able to go a step further by contacting document delivery suppliers for you and ordering the full text of articles that are going to be of value to you or your organization.

The effect of intelligent agents on the information profession

At first sight, intelligent agents may appear to threaten the traditional role of the information provider. After all, if a piece of software can be trained to locate appropriate information for the end-user and deliver it direct to the screen, how can the professional hope to compete?

However, I do not feel that the situation is actually as clear-cut as this. Intelligent agents are still at a very early phase in their development, and they can still provide inexplicable results. For example, I trained one agent to provide me with all the latest information on the football team that I follow (those readers with sharp eyes will know that it is Everton Football Club), and the agent returned with a series of results, most of which dealt with Formula One motor racing! So the term 'intelligent' is still something of a misnomer, and it is going to be a long time before agents are actually able to carry out complex searches with a high degree of accuracy.

Furthermore, in order to ensure that the agent produces high-quality results, considerable 'training' has to take place. The intelligent newspapers can only really provide a rough guide to overall areas of interest, and intelligent search engines require a lot of work to produce a tightly focused set of results. They are very time-consuming, and it is unlikely that they will appeal to busy end-users who simply want results quickly. They do have a very important role to play within an information service, however, and may prove to be an important addition in the information professional's armoury when it comes to providing a current awareness or selective dissemination service.

Summary

The benefits of intelligent agents are clear:

- The agents reduce the time taken searching the Internet for information.
- They can re-run searches for you on a regular basis.
- They overcome the problem of sorting out the new material from a mass of Web pages which have already been looked at in the past.
- The material that they retrieve is almost always going to be relevant.
- The user does not need to learn about search techniques and methods, or explore the intricacies of browsing and monitoring newsgroups.
- If a company is running an intranet they do not need to institute complicated methods of ensuring that the employees see important documents or information, since their agents will immediately inform them of new data as soon as it is made available.
- Virtual communities of users can easily be created, allowing enhanced sharing of information.
- Updated information can be displayed on a personalized Web page for you, allowing immediate access to the data itself via hypertext links.
- Agents continue to work even when you have gone home for the night, preparing updated information ready for viewing when you arrive at work the next morning.
- Intelligent agents allow you to set up a number of profiles which may be subject-specific or designed for particular individuals or groups.

URLs mentioned in this chapter

http://www.chatter-bots.com
http://www.filmfinder.com/
http://www.shoppingexplore.com
http://www.crayon.net
http://www.agentware.com
http://www.yahoo.com
http://www.excite.com
http://www.personal.lycos.com
http://www.wired.com/newbot/personal_agent.html
http://www.pointcast.com
http://www.qdeck.com
http://www.alexa.com

9

Usenet newsgroups and mailing lists

Introduction

The Internet is useful for many things, but perhaps it is best used for communication, either between individuals or groups of people. E-mail was the first implementation of this, but it is limited in what it can provide. What was also required was a method of passing information between groups of people, all of whom shared the same interests, whether academic or personal. Two methods have been introduced, Usenet newsgroups and mailing lists. This chapter discusses the similarities and differences between them, how to make use of them, and the advantages that they can give you as an information professional.

Usenet newsgroups.

I expect that you have heard of Usenet newsgroups, though you may have heard them described as any of the following: Usenet, newsgroups, netnews, discussion groups, or just news. For simplicity, I'll refer to them as newsgroups, but it is worth pointing out that, while they do carry a lot of news and current events information, that is not their only purpose. Newsgroups initially started life as far back as 1980 when two students in North Carolina established a method of transferring up to a dozen messages per day from one machine to another using something called UUCP (UNIX to UNIX Copy). These messages could be read by all the users who logged onto the system, and they could respond to the messages by posting their own, which would be copied back to the other machine.

Over the course of time this system was expanded; because the messages dealt with different topics, a hierarchy was introduced, allowing people to post to specific newsgroups, to ensure that users did not have to wade through all the messages just to find the two or three which interested them. Newsgroups have become an ever expanding area of the Internet – today there are over 50,000 newsgroups, and the posts to newsgroups add up to over 1 gigabyte per day. This has been doubling every year, and there are now over 24,000,000 people who participate in newsgroups. Usenet is now the largest public-information resource in the world and it is estimated that it is up to four times the size of the Web.

The method used to send newsgroup messages (commonly referred to as posts or postings) around the world is quite simple: a user posts a message to a particular newsgroup, usually using a piece of software called a newsreader (although it is now possible to post messages directly from the Web). This message is sent onwards to their Internet service provider's news server. The news server in turn copies the messages it has received to other news servers around the world, thus allowing other users to log onto their provider's news server, download the post and read it. They can then, if they choose, respond to the posts that interest them, and the whole process starts again. This is generally referred to as 'propagation', and as you can see, it is continual, with people seeing posts, responding to them, having them copied around the world and so on. As with most things to do with the Internet, it is a 24-hour-a-day, 365-days-of-the-year activity.

I mentioned earlier that newsgroups are split into hierarchies, and a newsgroup name is composed of several different elements separated by dots. There is what is known as the 'big seven' hierarchy, and the top level of these seven subject areas are as follows:

- **comp.** topics related to computing
- **misc.** miscellaneous topics that don't sit anywhere else in the hierarchy
- **news.** topics that relate to the Internet as a whole
- **rec.** recreational subjects, such as hobbies, sports, the arts and so on
- **sci.** anything to do with scientific subjects
- **soc.** social newsgroups, both social interaction and social

interests
- **talk.** which generally covers political issues.

Postings to these newsgroups are generally propagated to all news servers around the world, but there are also other newsgroups that are only of interest to particular regions, or that are regarded as rather more frivolous than the big seven. Examples of these are:

- **alt.** alternative, often controversial, subjects
- **bionet.** subjects of interest to biologists
- **uk.** subjects which may be of interest to people based in, or interested in, the UK.

There are a large number of other groups as well – these are just a few examples. Later in this chapter I'll explain how you can get a full list of newsgroups and choose the ones that you may find useful. For now, however, let's look a little further into the way that a newsgroup is named, with a few examples:

comp.infosystems.www.authoring.html
comp.os.ms–windows.apps.utilities.win95
misc.education
misc.misc
news.admin.censorship
news.announce.newusers
rec.pets.cats.health+behav
rec.skiing.resorts.europe
sci.physics.fusion
sci.space.shuttle
soc.culture.swiss
soc.history.war.us–civil–war
talk.abortion
talk.politics.mideast
uk.local.london
uk.media.tv.misc
alt.drugs
alt.books.iain–banks

You can see from the above examples (which were not entirely drawn at random; I have taken some of these groups myself!) that there is little by the way of a structure to the groups. Almost the only thing I can say is that they start from the general and move to the specific, but otherwise there is little overall consistency to be found. One of the reasons for this is that there is not a great deal of control over the establishment of a newsgroup, although there is a set procedure that must be adhered to in the creation of a newsgroup in the big seven, which requires that a proposition must be made and voted upon. In general terms, however, anyone can set up a newsgroup if enough people think that it is a good idea.

Most newsgroups are entirely open, which is to say that anyone can post a message to them, and although these postings are supposed to be 'on topic' to the group in question, this does not always happen. Most newsgroups do, however, have a charter, which is a statement defining what sort of posts are appropriate to the group. A small number of newsgroups are 'moderated', which means that, before a post is made available to news servers around the world, someone checks the message for content, validity and so on, and will only clear it for propagation if it satisfies the criteria which have previously been established.

Many newsgroups also have a FAQ, or Frequently Asked Questions list, which lists common questions and answers that people have posted to the newsgroup in the past. They can be a very useful source of information, and are usually posted about once every two weeks.

The value of newsgroups to information professionals

The posts that you find in newsgroups are an eclectic mixture of fact, fiction, rumour, advertisements and opinion. Most newsgroups are not moderated, so anyone can post anything that they like to them. In most cases posts are on-topic (that is to say, they are relevant to the subject area of the newsgroup), but sometimes people will spam newsgroups with inappropriate posts. Consequently, it can take some time to sort out the useful information from the nonsense that gets posted. This depends on the number of posts a

HINTS AND TIPS

Only subscribe to a small number of newsgroups in one go until you find out how busy they are, otherwise you may come in the next day to find thousands of posts waiting to be read!

DID YOU KNOW?

FAQ is usually pronounced to rhyme with 'back', but you may also hear it spelled out as F-A-Q.

newsgroup gets every day; some low-volume newsgroups will only get 2 or 3 posts in an average day, while other newsgroups, especially some in the **comp.** hierarchy will get over 500 posts per day.

However, it is worthwhile stressing that there is a lot of useful information to be gained from different newsgroups – the bug in the original Intel Pentium chip was reported to appropriate newsgroups, and the discussion which then took place encouraged Intel to respond to the problem quickly . Many businesses such as Microsoft, Blockbuster Video and Apple regularly monitor newsgroups, and are increasingly using them as a first-line method of communicating with users.

Individuals both pose and answer questions in newsgroups, debates take place, information is shared, new information is made available to each group's user community and details on new Web sites, conferences and exhibitions are regularly posted. Consequently, although the data held in newsgroups is often more opinion than fact, it can be a very useful place to begin researching a subject. Indeed, when I was writing this book, one of the first places where I looked for information on intelligent agents was in newsgroups, and I got some high-quality data, as well as lists of Web sites to visit.

One word of warning here, I'm afraid. If you post to newsgroups, within a short space of time you will begin to get unsolicited commercial e-mails (UCE for short) offering anything from the chance to get rich quickly through to cures for baldness. This is because unscrupulous companies skim newsgroups for e-mail addresses, which they then sell on to other people who send out UCE. There is very little you can do about this, and although some people alter their e-mail addresses when posting to newsgroups this is a poor solution at best.

Reading newsgroups

Having whetted your appetite for newsgroups, I'll now explain how you can use them. There are basically three ways of doing this: general search engines, Web-based utilities and software packages.

DID YOU KNOW?

No one can say for certain why the term 'spam' became used for inappropriate postings. However, it seems likely that it is related to the Monty Python Spam sketch, in which Spam is in every item on the menu, and it is impossible to order anything without having at least some of it included in the meal.

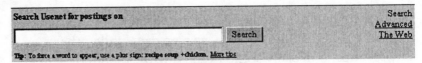

Fig. 9.1   *Searching Usenet using AltaVista*

General search engines

We have already seen that, in order to increase the number of people using search engines, their owners are constantly increasing their functionality. It is now becoming common to be able to search newsgroups using the same engines that you would normally search the Web with. The AltaVista default is to search the Web, but in the right-hand corner of the search box there is an option to search Usenet instead, and Figure 9.1 illustrates the screen which is then displayed. This leads to a set of results which give information on any posts that contain the requested search term(s), as shown in Figure 9.2.

However, the disadvantage of this approach is that the

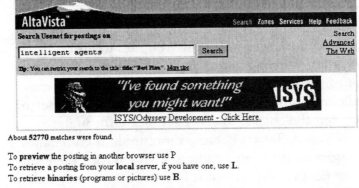

Fig. 9.2   *The result of an AltaVista search in Usenet for intelligent agents*

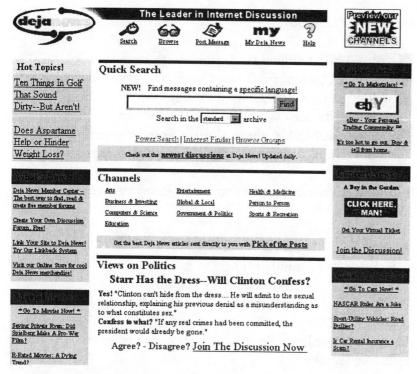

Fig. 9.3   *The Deja News search interface*

functionality is limited, and not all newsgroups are available. If you have a serious interest in searching newsgroups you may therefore find it more productive to use one of the other methods described below.

Web based utilities

On the Web, probably the best-known utility for searching newsgroups is a search engine called Deja News, which can be found at **http://www.dejanews.com**. It is a very specialized search engine, because all it does is to search newsgroups for you; it doesn't search the Web as AltaVista does, for example.

The opening screen of Deja News is shown in Figure 9.3. Deja News is one of the most powerful and sophisticated search engines on the Web. You can input your search terms directly into the Find box, and Deja News will attempt to find all references to the requested information across all the newsgroups.

Deja News allows searchers to use standard Boolean operators (see Chapter 3).

- ◼ 'phil AND bradley' finds posts with both words
- ◼ 'phil OR philip' finds posts with one word or the other
- ◼ 'classification AND NOT cataloguing' finds posts which contain the first word but not the second
- ◼ 'president NEAR clinton' finds posts containing both words, in either order, within 5 words of each other

If preferred, the operators can be replaced by symbols as follows:

AND	phil & bradley
OR	phil | philip
AND NOT	classification &! cataloguing
NEAR	president ^ clinton

It is also possible to use other symbols to create an even more effective search:

^ 20	finds two words within 20 words of each other
"phrase searching"	using quotation marks for a phrase search
librar*	wildcard (library, libraries, librarian)
place?	wildcard for one character (i.e. places, placed but not placebo)
captain & (kirk | picard)	forces the bracketed expression to be evaluated first

It is also possible to search for

An author	~a philb@twilight.demon.co.uk
A subject	~s soccer
A newsgroup	~g rec.pets.cats
Creation date of article	~dc 1997/10/31

Alternatively, you can make use of the Power Search feature that is shown in Figure 9.4. This allows a greater degree of flexibility, and you can specify restrictions on the search such

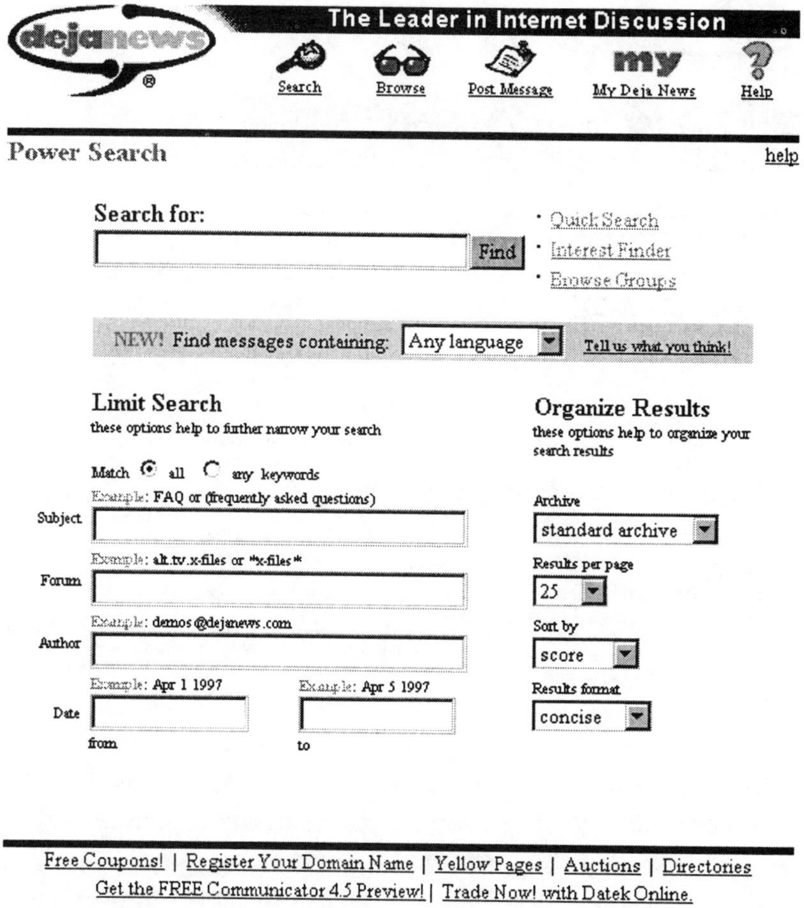

The Leader in Internet Discussion

dejanews ®

Search   Browse   Post Message   My Deja News   Help

Power Search

help

Search for:

[   ] Find

- Quick Search
- Interest Finder
- Browse Groups

NEW! Find messages containing: [Any language ▾] Tell us what you think!

Limit Search
these options help to further narrow your search

Match ● all ○ any keywords

Example: FAQ or (frequently asked questions)

Subject [   ]

Example: alt.tv.x-files or *x-files*

Forum [   ]

Example: demos@dejanews.com

Author [   ]

Example: Apr 1 1997   Example: Apr 5 1997

Date [   ]   [   ]
     from   to

Organize Results
these options help to organize your search results

Archive
[standard archive ▾]

Results per page
[25 ▾]

Sort by
[score ▾]

Results format
[concise ▾]

Free Coupons! | Register Your Domain Name | Yellow Pages | Auctions | Directories
Get the FREE Communicator 4.5 Preview! | Trade Now! with Datek Online.

Fig. 9.4   *Deja News Power Search options*

as subject, date, author, full or partial match of keywords, newsgroups searched in, and how the results are to be displayed back to. Once the search has been run, Deja News will display a screen similar to that shown in Figure 9.5. On the left-hand side is the date the message was posted to the newsgroup, next to that is Scr (score) rating the relevance of the article from 1 to 100; the higher the score, the more relevant the posting. In the middle of the screen is the subject of the posting, next is the name of the newsgroup it was posted to, and on the right-hand side is the name of the author.

The information given is not as extensive as might be wished, but there is a limit to the amount of information that can be displayed on the screen. However, it is the matter of a few moments to click on the subject heading and display the

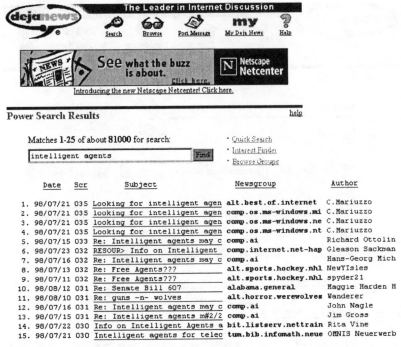

Fig. 9.5   *Results of a Deja News search*

full posting on the screen. An example of this step is shown in Figure 9.6 (I've disguised the name of the individual who originally posted the question for their privacy).

As you can see, there are a variety of different options available to you from this screen, and a good understanding of them will ensure that searching for information becomes even faster and more effective. When you view the posting, any URLs contained within it will be displayed as an active link, which is very useful, as you can simply click on the link and go directly to the appropriate Web page. In my opinion, this is one of the strongest features of Deja News, as it really does speed up locating useful sites to visit.

Options are available to allow you to move back to a previous article, on to the next article in the thread, or to view the thread in its entirety. This is useful because it allows quick scanning in order to find answers to particular questions, or to follow a particular line of discussion.

Deja News also encourages interaction, and it is possible to subscribe to the particular newsgroup, to post articles to the group or to e-mail the poster directly.

```
Subject:      Re: ftp: binary or ascii
From:         Phil Bradley <philb@twilight.demon.co.uk>
Date:         1998/04/23
Message-ID:   <CeaCoBA0a4P1EwVr@twilight.demon.co.uk>
Newsgroups:   demon.homepages.authoring
[More Headers]

[Subscribe to demon.homepages.authoring]


In article <Psh$MKA2I1P1Iweh@wholehog.demon.co.uk>, 粉某某 某某某,
<某某某@某某某.demon.co.uk> writes
>what's the difference between ASCII mode and BINARY mode, and when
>should I use them?
>
>ASCII for HTML text, BINARY for images and zips?
I upload everything in binary and have never had a problem.

Phil.
--
Phil Bradley: Internet Consultant, Trainer, Web designer and Author.
Visit http://www.philb.com for free information on Internet Introductions,
search engine articles, web design tips and a host of other free information.
** New! Going Online, CD-ROM and the Internet. Published in December 1997 **
```

Fig. 9.6   *Deja News display of one of my posts to a Web authoring group*

One final very valuable feature is the opportunity to view the posting profile of the author of the post that is being viewed. There are a number of reasons why this is useful: it allows you to identify people who are expert in a particular area, to locate lost friends or colleagues, and to track what individuals are saying and doing on newsgroups. There is of course a privacy issue involved here, but Deja News does have a policy whereby posters can ensure that their postings are not archived. To give you an example of what an author profile looks like, I've used mine, and you can see the partial results in Figure 9.7 (the Spice Girls reference was because I replied to a post which was crossposted to that group; it is not one that I frequent myself). This is not necessarily an entirely accurate indication of the activities of a poster, since many messages will be cross-posted to a number of different newsgroups; however, it is a fairly good indication of the author's main interests.

By now, it should come as no surprise that Deja News has

HINTS AND TIPS

Remember that most of the information you will retrieve from newsgroups is opinions, rather than facts, so be careful of just relying on such information; check other sources as well.

Author Profile

Author: Phil Bradley <philb@twilight.demon.co.uk>

- 340 unique articles posted.
- Number of articles posted to individual newsgroups (slightly skewed by to cross-postings):

  - 151 demon.homepages.authoring
  - 64 soc.libraries.talk
  - 34 rec.arts.sf.fandom
  - 21 uk.media.tv.misc
  - 10 uk.people.sf-fans
  - 7 alt.books.iain-banks
  - 6 alt.homepages.designtips.uk
  - 6 bit.listserv.cdromlan
  - 6 uk.consultants
  - 5 rec.arts.sf.written
  - 4 alt.tv.simpsons
  - 4 uk.misc
  - 2 rec.pets.cats.health+behav
  - 2 uk.media.tv.time-team
  - 2 uk.net
  - 1 alt.music.spice-girls
  - 1 alt.tv.space-a-n-b
  - 1 alt.war.civil.usa
  - 1 demon.homepages.adverts
  - 1 demon.ip.support.turnpike
  - 1 misc.education.language.english

Fig. 9.7   *My Deja News author profile*

created a 'My Deja News' service, which does for newsgroups what 'My Yahoo!' has done for the Web in general. 'My Deja News' is a free service, and one which can be set up within a matter of a few minutes. It allows you to establish a profile based on particular interests, to subscribe to particular newsgroups, read the postings from them and also to post directly to the newsgroups you are interested in. It is also valuable in that, because the profile is held on a Deja News server, rather than on a local hard disk, you can use it wherever you happen to be. This is very useful if you spend a lot of time on the move, but still wish to keep up to date with what is happening in a particular set of newsgroups.

The disadvantage of this approach, however, is that it is necessary to be online when reading and posting articles.

Newsgroups can take up a frightening amount of time, so if you connect to the Internet using a dial-up modem connection this might become an expensive way of reading newsgroups. To give you a quick example, I currently subscribe to about twenty newsgroups, and I spend at least one hour a day reading and responding to posts. If I had to do all this with an online connection I would very quickly run into financial problems, and this is where offline newsreaders become very important.

Offline newsreaders

A possible solution to the problem of online costs is to make use of an offline newsreader. The utilities work in a similar fashion to Deja News, in that you are able to obtain a list of all of the newsgroups, decide on the ones that are of interest and subscribe to them. The difference is in how the information is delivered. You log onto the Internet and start the offline newsreader, which connects to the Internet service provider and downloads all the new posts onto the local hard disk. (Offline newsreaders can usually also be configured to just downloading the subject headings).

You are then able to read the postings offline at leisure, and can take as much time as you wish to write responses to posts, check any information and so on. Once you are happy with the responses you have written, you can log back onto the Internet and the offline reader will send the postings to the news server.

There are a great many different offline newsreaders available, and a comprehensive list of them can be found at **http://www.yahoo.com/Computers_and_Internet/ Software/Internet/Usenet**. They all work in a similar fashion; the one that I'll concentrate on here is called Forte Free Agent, which can be downloaded from **http://www. forteinc.com**. It is simple and fast to use, and – as the name implies – it is also free, although there is a commercial version, Agent 1.5, which has greater functionality.

The main screen is shown in Figure 9.8. The screen is divided into three main windows: Subscribed Groups, subject headings, and the text of the selected article.

Free Agent is quick to configure, in that all you need to do

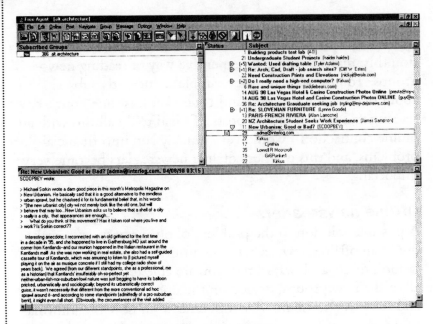

Fig. 9.8   *The Forte Free Agent interface*

is to give it the address of your Internet service provider's news server. It then visits the server and downloads a list of all the newsgroups the news server takes; if the ISP takes a full news feed this may take some time, since Free Agent has to obtain a list of tens of thousands of newsgroups for you.

You can then browse the list of newsgroups and select the ones you are interested in receiving. Free Agent can then go online and download a list of subject headers for you. You can then choose (simply by clicking on the header) to retrieve the whole article there and then to read, or if you prefer, you can do this offline, marking the articles you are interested in. When you next log on, Free Agent can download these articles to your hard disk, and you can read them later at your leisure.

Free Agent, in common with other newsreaders, will allow you to follow particular threads, post your own articles or responses to others, and download images and display them on the screen for you.

Mailing lists
Mailing lists (also called discussion lists or listservs) are very

similar to newsgroups in concept, but they work quite differently in practice, and this leads to an entirely distinct atmosphere. As we have already seen, newsgroups require newsreading software, or a visit to a Web site such as Deja News. Mailing lists work by using e-mail. Instead of posting via Deja News or Free Agent (for example), you send an e-mail with the text of your message to another e-mail account held on a server somewhere around the world. That server is responsible for sending your e-mail onto everyone else who subscribes to the mailing list. Your message then arrives in their e-mail box, and if they wish to reply, they can send you e-mail directly, post back to the mailing list for everyone else to see, or do both.

Characteristics of mailing lists

As you can see from the preceding paragraph, the principle of mailing lists is the same as that of newsgroups – a group of people communicating with each other. However, as the system works using e-mail, there are a number of quite substantial differences in the way in which information professionals can make use of it.

Joining a mailing list is also slightly different to joining a newsgroup. You can join a newsgroup by simply selecting it from the list presented by Free Agent or Deja News, as we have discussed, but to join a mailing list you need to send a message to an appropriate e-mail address requesting to join it. (I'll cover this process in more detail below.) Although this is not exactly a big hurdle it does require a little extra effort, and as a result individuals who simply want to advertise their products, usually but not always related to some aspect of sexual activity, tend to ignore mailing lists. As a result, the traffic is reduced and the posts are more focused, although this does of course vary with individual groups and lists.

Mailing lists always have an owner, usually the person who set it up. The owner plays an important role in defining the nature and atmosphere of the list by deciding what subjects should be discussed, whether certain types of post (announcements for example) are permitted, and limiting discussion on a topic if it is felt that it has continued for too long. The owner may also decide if the list should be moder-

HINTS AND TIPS

A general rule of thumb is that you will find more serious and accurate information from a mailing list rather than from a newsgroup, although this is not always the case. Please remember that, as with newsgroups, much of what is posted is opinion, not fact.

ated or not. A moderated list means that each post has to be checked by the owner, and only if the post is approved as appropriate will it be passed on for all members to read it. This is another major difference from most newsgroups, which anyone can post to, saying whatever they wish. A moderated list will generally be kept much more on track, with a smaller number of daily postings. The slight danger of a moderated list is that the list owner is all-powerful, and may delete postings for any number of reasons. This could result in rather a bland series of posts, particularly in mailing lists established by commercial organizations for discussion of their products, since the moderator may decide to delete postings which are critical. However, members of a list in which this occurs generally realize quickly what's going on and unsubscribe. Finally, because moderation is time-consuming there may be a considerable delay between a post being sent and its being seen by the list members.

Locating mailing lists

Unfortunately, there is no single comprehensive list of mailing lists, so it might be necessary to do a little research in order to find lists that are of interest. However, there are some very good resources on the Web that can assist in this.

Liszt

Perhaps the largest single listing can be found at Liszt, **http://www.liszt.com**, which provides details on about 90,000 mailing lists. Liszt arranges the mailing lists using a broad subject category approach while offering a basic search facility. This is simple to use and very effective; it should be a matter of a few moments to locate appropriate lists. Information is also available on most of the lists, giving you the opportunity to check on the subject matter before joining it.

PAML

A second useful resource is PAML, or Publicly Available Mailing Lists, which is to be found at **http://www.neosoft. com/internet/paml/default.html**. This is also a large list, with details of over 2,700 lists available. To give you an indication of the breadth of coverage of the lists, I've included

Publicly Accessible Mailing Lists

Sponsors? Look here!

• • • • • • • • • • •

Names

<u>0</u> [A] <u>B</u> <u>C</u> <u>D</u> <u>E</u> <u>F</u> <u>G</u> <u>H</u> <u>I</u> <u>J</u> <u>K</u> <u>L</u> <u>M</u> <u>N</u> <u>O</u> <u>P</u> <u>Q</u> <u>R</u> <u>S</u> <u>T</u> <u>U</u> <u>V</u> <u>W</u> <u>X</u> <u>Y</u> <u>Z</u>

```
a-ha                    A-INFOS                 A-List
A-PARENTS-CHINA         a-parents-vietnam       A.Word.A.Day
AA-MDS-TALK             AA Men's Meeting        AACRL
AADD-FOCUSED            AAF                     AAIH
AANEWS                  abaa-announcements      abbeyweb
ABC                     abdsurvivalguide-list   ABEILLES
ABERNATHY               abolition-caucus        aboutherbs
ABPART-L                AbundantBible           ACCESS-L
accra-commresrch        accra-econdev           ACCRI-L
ACHD                    ACHD-P                  acid-jazz
acim                    acimlessons             acimwkbk
AClist                  ACORN-L                 acoustiCDiscussion
acoustic guitar         Acrobat                 act-mtl
ACTING-L                activeds                ACTNOW-L
ACTVST-L                acudetox-1              Acupuncture-L
ad-bytes                ada-belgium             ada-belgium-info
ADA-Law                 Adaptec CDR             add-holistic
ADD-Mate                ADDCTNSG                ADDICT-L
Addiction Topics        ADDISONS                addparents
```

Fig. 9.9   *PAML alphabetical listing of mailing lists*

part of the page listing mailing lists alphabetically in Figure 9.9.

A full list of mailing lists that PAML is aware of can be obtained either directly from the site, or from **ftp://rtfm. mit.edu/pub/usenet-by-group/news.lists.misc/**, and it is also posted on a monthly basis to the newsgroup **news.lists.misc**. Please be aware, however, that the full listing is so large it is split into 20 different postings.

Mailbase

The final resource is one called Mailbase based in the UK at **http://www.mailbase.ac.uk** This service is funded by JISC (Joint Information System Committee, **http://www.jisc. ac.uk**), and as a result the focus of the lists is centred on the UK (particularly, though not exclusively, subjects of interest to British academic staff and information professionals), although people from other countries are not excluded from joining Mailbase lists. In fact it has almost 2,000 lists with over 134,000 subscribers worldwide. Figure 9.10 illustrates the opening screen at Mailbase.

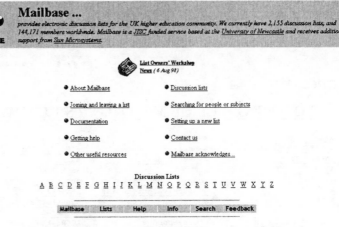

Fig. 9.10   *The Mailbase home page*

Appropriate lists can be found by looking through the alphabetical list, though a more effective method of locating them is to use the search facility offered by Mailbase. Once you have located a list which is of interest, you can check through the information that is available on it, such as the members and the number of postings per month, and you can search the archives of the list as well. This will give you a better idea of the subject content and how busy the list is. The last point here is important; if you subscribe to too many busy lists you will spend all day reading e-mail and doing nothing else!

Joining, leaving and posting to mailing lists

All of the resources that I've mentioned so far will give you precise details on how to join, leave and post to a mailing list, and you should keep this information safe for future reference. I'll use as an example a mailing list at Mailbase called lis-link, which has been established for library and information science professionals in higher education and research institutions in the UK and elsewhere. The commands used are specific to this mailing list, but the principle is the same, regardless of the list you join and wherever it might happen to be.

To subscribe to this list you send an e-mail to **mailbase@mailbase.ac.uk** with the message: join lis-link Firstname Lastname. To leave the list you send an e-mail to the same address with the message: leave lis-link.

These commands are sent directly to the computer that is responsible for administering the list, and it will be able to add you to the list or delete you from the list immediately. However, this e-mail address (**mailbase@mailbase.ac.uk**) is not the address to which you send messages to be sent out to list members. The address for this is **lis-link@mailbase. ac.uk** It is important that you send messages to the correct e-mail address, because if you send a message to leave the list to **lis-link@mailbase.ac.uk** it will automatically be distributed to everyone on the list and you will end up looking rather silly!

Some guidelines on posting to newsgroups and mailing lists

If you are an experienced subscriber to newsgroups or mailing lists you may wish to skip this section, since you will already have discovered by observation, or trial and error, most of the things that I mention.

Newsgroups and mailing lists can be a very useful way of obtaining information, and a few minutes research using Deja News or searching the archives of a mailing list may answer your question. On the other hand, you may wish to get more involved than just reading the newsgroups or mailing lists and decide to start posting, either to ask questions yourself or to try and answer those asked by others. The following are a few pointers that should hopefully make your introduction to newsgroups and mailing lists enjoyable and painless.

- Read the newsgroup/mailing list for at least a few days, and preferably a few weeks, before you start posting yourself. Each newsgroup is its own little community, complete with helpful and knowledgeable people, others who like nothing more than to pick an argument, and still more who enjoy causing problems. Take some time to learn who is who; that way you will quickly see whose posts are worth reading, and those posters that you can safely ignore.
- Read the FAQ before you start asking questions. Most

newsgroups and mailing lists publish a FAQ, or Frequently Asked Questions, once every two weeks, or perhaps monthly. The FAQ, as the name implies, is a compilation of those questions that are asked frequently. To save people time having to answer the same questions over and over, the FAQ does this instead. It is quite likely that the question you want to ask has already been answered, and a quick check will confirm this; most importantly, it will stop you looking like an idiot!

■ Do not advertise. Only a very small number of newsgroups or mailing lists allow overt advertising. If you post an advertisement to a group which does not want them, you will find your mailbox quickly filling up with messages from people who will tell you (sometimes politely, sometimes not) that advertisements are not wanted.

■ Think about your post before you send it. It is very easy to write and send a post to a newsgroup in the heat of the moment, and if you post when you are angry you will doubtless say things you will regret later. If you are really angry, do not post a response until the next day when you have calmed down and can think rationally and objectively about what you want to say.

■ Don't get involved in a 'flamewar'. This is a situation in which two or more people who hold different views start posting abusive comments to each other in the newsgroup. Flamewars are unhelpful, they do not add anything to a newsgroup and the only result is that you may get a reputation for being an offensive, childish poster, and people will ignore anything you have to say.

■ Ensure that your posts are appropriate to the newsgroup. There is no point in sending a post about the latest HTML tag to **rec.pets.cats**, since the readers of the newsgroup will have no interest in the subject and will be unlikely to respond to your post in a positive manner.

■ Resist the impulse to 'spam' or cross-post your message. If you post a message to a number of different newsgroups or mailing lists, people who take them will see multiple copies of your message, and if they reply their message will be copied widely in return, leading to a mess of postings across groups.

- When writing, choose a sensible subject heading that clearly describes the content of your post. Subscribers do not generally read every single post and use the headings of the posts to decide which ones to read. You are more likely to get a response if your heading says 'Help needed installing Netscape version 4.x on Win 95' instead of just 'Help'.

- Don't quote an entire message when you reply. Keep your responses short and to the point, and only quote short sections of the original posting that you are commenting on.

- If you ask a question in a newsgroup, try to answer one from someone else. This isn't a requirement, or even standard practice, but it does help to make the newsgroup a useful, informative and pleasant place to spend time.

Summary

- Newsgroups and mailing lists are a valuable way of keeping up to date with what is happening in a particular subject area.

- They allow information professionals to keep in touch with each other, to share and swap experiences, and to ask and answer questions.

- They can take up considerable amounts of time, and require thought and tact if your experiences there are to be positive ones.

URLs mentioned in this chapter

http://www.yahoo.com/Computers_and_Internet/
    Software/Internet/Usenet
http://www.forteinc.com
http://www.dejanews.com
http://www.liszt.com
http://www.neosoft.com/internet/paml/default.html
ftp://rtfm.mit.edu/pub/usenet-by-group/
    news.lists.misc/
http://www.mailbase.ac.uk
http://www.jisc.ac.uk

Part 3

The future

10

The information mix and into the future

Introduction

I hope that you have found the previous chapters useful and informative, but I am aware that so far I have treated elements such as search engines and intelligent agents as largely as discrete utilities. Of course, when searching the Internet on a daily this is an unrealistic way to approach the question 'how do I find the best and most relevant information quickly?', since the best way of obtaining what you need is generally to use a combination of different resources.

In this chapter I attempt to merge all the different elements into a coherent whole, using some real examples of Internet searching. I also cover a number of other elements related to searching which I have included so far, and finally take a quick look into my crystal ball to highlight possible future technologies.

A quick glance through this chapter, with its many references to information professionals, might lead you to think that unless you have that sort of background it is not relevant to you. This is certainly not the case, and I'd like to emphasize that anyone may need to find the sort of information that I have referred to in my examples. Furthermore, you may not work in a library or use one each day, but you probably have a collection of books at home, and will find some of my points pertinent to the decisions you make about what to buy or how to arrange them.

Where do I go first?

You now have a large array of tools at your disposal which should make the task of searching the Internet rather easier. At this point, however, I suspect that you may be a little bewildered, since you have so much choice and so many starting points! You might well be thinking 'Should I use a search engine, and if so, which one? How about an intelligent agent instead? Or should I ask in a newsgroup? Or on a mailing list?'

To begin with, let's go back to basics. If you are finding information for an end-user, the initial approach is no different from any other reference enquiry you receive, and if you are looking for information for yourself you will have to ask similar questions:

- Has the user clearly identified what information he/she wants?
- Are there any synonyms you should be aware of, particularly when searching global resources? – the term 'football' means very different things depending on which side of the Atlantic you live.
- Does the user require a very specific piece of information, or an overview of a subject?
- Does the information have to be 'official'? In other words, what level of authority does the user require?
- Does the information have to be current, and if so, current to today, last week or last month?
- What format does the user want? Text, a moving image, a picture, or perhaps a sound file?
- Does the information have to be in a particular language?
- Is the user prepared to pay for the information, or does it have to be free?
- Is the information needed once only, or is it part of an ongoing project, requiring frequent updates?

These are just a few of the questions that you need to be clear on before you can begin your search; I'm sure that you ask many of them at the moment, and probably some more besides. However, when using the Internet to answer queries you have many more resources available, and it is not difficult to work out from the list above which questions relate specifically to that, rather than to the more traditional searching which you have been doing in the past.

Once you have obtained answers to as many of these questions as possible, you are in a position to begin structuring your search. It seems an obvious point, but it is one which is nonetheless worth making – can you find the answer using another resource? It is very tempting always to think of the Internet, but an effective searcher requires the answer, and should not be over-concerned about the way the answer is obtained. If you can point the user towards a book, or the back-run of a journal, or pull a reference book off the shelf and obtain the answer that way, that is just as effective, if not more so, than logging onto the Internet, starting your browser, choosing a search engine, running the search, locating an appropriate site, waiting until it is displayed on the screen, scrolling down and eventually finding the particular fact required!

Some sample searches
Using an index search engine

However, for this purpose I will assume that you have already thought of using local resources, but have decided that using the Internet is the best way of searching for the required data. We'll take as our first example a situation in which you have to locate current developments in teaching children with dyslexia. A search for the term 'dyslexia' in Yahoo! provides us with two categories for the disability:

Society and Culture: Disabilities: Specific Disabilities: Learning Disabilities: Dyslexia

Regional: Countries: United Kingdom: Society and Culture: Disabilities: Specific Disabilities: Learning Disabilities: Dyslexia

and a total of 82 sites. The first site that I tried (a treatment centre for dyslexia) was unavailable, but the second site, the Medical Dyslexia and A.D.D. Treatment Center (**http://www.dyslexiaonline.com/center.html**) provided me with lots of information about the subject, including an introduction, a list of publications and information on medical treatment. The Center's page was updated three days prior to my visit and is maintained by someone who (according to the site) has published widely in the field. If I was in any doubt I could now visit Amazon.com just to check this, and obtain a list of the titles he has published. However, at this point I am satisfied with the authority of the site in question. The page provides me with a link back to the home page for the site, which among other things displays an animation of a poem written by a student suffering from dyslexia, which then changes into a picture of the poem after he was treated. While this does not provide hard factual information it does graphically show the difference which treatment can make. Of course, I could have seen the same 'before and after' images in a book, but I'm sure they would have had far less impact.

Although I could stop my search at that point, I thought it was worth going back to Yahoo! to see what other sites they had available, and found several others, all providing me with appropriate information. I was also able to locate the Web sites of several dyslexia associations and institutes. The whole search took no more than 3 or 4 minutes from launching my browser. Of course, if I wanted more information I could have followed a variety of other avenues, but since I had the answer to my query I decided to stop at that point.

Finding a film quotation

Another enquiry, of a slightly different nature this time. Someone wanted to know if the well known phrase 'play it again Sam' was an accurate quote. Rather than running a search on a general search engine, I happened to know of the existence of the Internet Movie Database at **http://www. imdb.com** which is a superb resource for film and film-related information. One of the search options provided is a word search, with a further option for searching the database collection of quotes. 'Play it again Sam' is not listed, so I reduced the phrase to 'play it' and came up with ten references. It didn't take me long to find out that the actual quote was said by Rick Blaine to Sam in, of course, *Casablanca*. (Out of interest I went to AltaVista and ran a search on the phrase, to be faced with a total of over 3,000 documents.) I then decided that it might be a nice idea to see if I could obtain a sound file of the actual quote. An obvious place to look for this type of information would be a site which provides audio clips. The best way to locate such a site is to use a multi-search engine, and I chose to use Metaplus at **http://www.metaplus.com**. One of the results was a link to a site called the Daily .WAV at **http://www.dailywav.com/** (a .wav file is a type of audio file). This site provided me with access to six audio quotes from the film, but unfortunately not the one I was looking for. However, the site did point me to a 'sound ring'. A ring is simply a list of sites that have the same subject matter, each one links to the next. They can be quite useful, since they enable you to move from one site to another looking for appropriate data, although some luck is required! Rather than move around the ring, I moved to the home page of the sound ring at **http://sound-ring.com/index.html**. Following the links I located a personal home page which had the file, downloaded it, and so was able to listen to Bogart say the immortal line. I should point out that there are of course copyright implications in individuals archiving such material on their Web sites, and also regarding your own use of such material, so please do be careful before using data of this nature!

Using mailing lists to find a speaker

A third example now, and this time I want to find someone who would be a good speaker on a course that I'm running on electronic copyright and legal issues related to the Internet. Since the course is running in the UK, they have to be geographically close. I decided to do a little lateral searching at this point. Good speakers often come from the world of academia, and are quite likely to post messages about the subjects they are interested in on mailing lists. Mailbase at **http://www.mailbase.ac.uk** came up with one list in particular, **law-www**, which covered the correct area, so I searched the archives for 'electronic copyright'. I retrieved a number of hits, several of which related to an online legal journal, and ten minutes of browsing that gave me a list of half a dozen potential speakers. I then referred back to the mailing list to see what messages they were posting, took a look at some of their personal pages on the Web, and was able to narrow down my shortlist and e-mail my preferred choices to see if they were able to speak on my course.

Finding factual information using reference books

I'll take one last example now, lest I bore you to distraction. A friend wanted to know how many airports there were in the UK, for reasons best known only to himself. I started by searching in AltaVista, limiting my search using the domain:uk qualifier and the term 'airports', but still came up with over 8,000 hits. I narrowed this down to four hits when I changed my search term to the phrase 'number of airports', but unfortunately when I looked at them I found that there was information on Russia and Australia (remember that domain:uk merely limits to sites based in the UK, not about the content of those sites); although one site did link to two journals, I was still unable to find the information I required. I then decided to visit the British Government home page at **http://www.open.gov.uk**. A search through the site listed over 1,000 documents that contained the words I was looking for. Deciding against that approach I located the Department of the Environment, Transport and the Regions, and their home page pointed me towards their page on statistics, which in turn listed a number of individuals and contact points for civil servants who may have been able to answer my question. At this point I seriously thought of calling a halt, but remembered that another search that I'd done recently on events in London led me to the *Time Out* site at **http://www.timeout.co.uk**. Rather than taking a direct approach, I wondered what other sites like *Time Out* might contain the information I required, so instead of running searches on the subject I was interested in, I started to look for sites which might contain the information; a subtle but important distinction.

I remembered from my days of working in the library that the CIA produced a useful world factbook, so it was only a matter of moments to locate it at **http://www.adci.gov/cia/publications/factbook/**, virtually flip to the section on the UK and scroll down to the section on Transportation, to find not only the number of airports (338), but also those with paved and unpaved runways of specific lengths! The only problem with the data was that it was based on 1995 figures, but that was good enough for my friend.

There are any number of different ways in which the above queries could have been answered, but hopefully these examples demonstrate that in most cases the best way to answer a query is to adopt a flexible approach and not to rely wholly on any one resource. I could also have spent a lot longer on each of the queries, and I might have found more information, or alternatively I could have searched for another hour only to find nothing more. The longer you are able to devote to searching the Internet, the more confident you become, and the easier it is to know when to call a halt.

The examples should also demonstrate that in some cases the Internet will not give you a final result, but will merely assist you on the journey. This is particularly the case when you think it is going to be necessary to talk to a real live person. In both the transport and copyright examples, the Internet led to contacts, enabling me to talk directly to individuals if I had wanted to. Indeed, I think one of the greatest strengths of the system is not just the amount of information it provides access to, or the currency of the information, but the way in which it can put you in touch with other people.

Incorporating the Internet into your overall information strategy

There are very few occasions when introducing the Internet will result in reduced subscriptions or the wholesale destruction of unnecessary materials. Let's look at a selection of resources to see how practical this is.

◼ **Newspapers**. All the large daily newspapers are now available on the Internet, and for most of them access is free, although some, such as the *Financial Times*, do charge for an archival service. Most newspapers do not, however, put their entire daily contents onto their Web sites – the *Daily Telegraph* at **http://www. telegraph.co.uk** only puts about 70% of each day's paper up on the Web, and there are significant omissions such as the Obituary column. If your information centre only requires current copies of the papers it is certainly worth checking to see if the subscriptions can be stopped, depending on the use which is made of them. Moreover, if you archive large back-runs of papers you may well find that it is worth disposing of them, since better search facilities can sometimes be provided by CD-ROM-based versions or by archival services from their Internet sites. This may turn out to be more expensive (certainly if others follow the *Financial Times* approach), but it may be a faster and more effective way of providing a service, along the 'just in time' rather than 'just in case' model.

■ **Encyclopaedias**. The value of encyclopaedias lies not only in the data, but also in the information held in photographs, charts and other graphical material. While all of this is certainly available with online versions, it will take a long time to download high quality images, even with fast connections. A better approach might be to invest in a CD-ROM version of the product and provide network access to it from around your internal network. If that is not possible, it may be best to stay with paper versions for the time being.

■ **Commercial databases**. As we saw in Chapter 6, many companies are now offering access via the Internet, rather than direct-dial access. Technically there is little difference between these two methods of access; both require software, telephone lines and modems. The crucial difference may lie in the different interfaces available, and generally the Web-based version will be easier and more straightforward for people to use. This can certainly be an incentive if you intend to allow your users to access such databases for themselves, although of course you might have to do some research to find out exactly how the billing structure differs. A small number of databases which have been made available commercially can also be searched free across the Internet, MEDLINE being one such example. However, although the data is the same as that contained in the commercial version, offers you may find that the Web interface is of inferior quality. CD-ROM versions could still prove to have value, particularly if the software provided allows users to interrogate both locally held resources and Internet-based resources at the same time. However, as with encyclopaedias, if much of the information is held in a graphical format it may still be better to keep up a CD-ROM-based subscription for the time being.

- **Yellow and white pages**. This is certainly one area in which I would suggest that the paper copy could be disposed of, though more so with the Yellow Pages than the White. Internet Yellow Pages allow much wider searches, based on company name, location and subject, with links to appropriate Web sites, and the paper-based versions, as well as taking up a lot of space, simply cannot match the ease and speed of use. White pages are a little more difficult, at least in the UK, since the body of information is carefully restricted. However, it may be worth doing some research for yourselves to discover if the online version is more comprehensive and current than the paper version. If that is the case you might discover you can save several feet of shelving.

- **Company annual reports**. It is becoming quite common for companies to put their entire annual reports on their Web sites, making them searchable and adding hypertext links. However, it is unlikely that they will be doing the same with older versions, so it might be necessary to hold onto the archival versions, while managing quite happily without the current versions.

- **Dictionaries**. Dictionaries can be searched faster and more effectively online than in a paper format, and may also help suggest appropriate words (in the same way that word-processors do) if you mis-spell the word you are looking for. An online dictionary can finally overcome the age-old problem of trying to check the spelling of a word when you need to know what the spelling is before you can do it!

- **Specific reference tools**. This of course depends on exactly what the reference tool is, and whether there is an Internet version available. One of the first things that I did when I got access to the Internet in my home was to throw away all my film- and movie-related reference works, because I knew that I could get better service from the Internet Movie Database. For good measure I also threw away almanacs, a copy of the Bible and so on, simply because I knew that I could find the information I need more quickly and easily using the Internet than by trying to hunt through a printed reference work.

■ **Official papers**. Governments are increasingly using the Internet to publish information such as papers, discussion documents, legal texts, press releases and so on. It is certainly worthwhile checking the Web sites of your own government and ministries in that hope that material you might otherwise have to purchase has been made available free of charge.

Information professionals unite! You have nothing to lose but your books...

I am sure that many of you, reading the above bullet points, will be reacting with horror at the idea of throwing away parts of your collections. However, I think this is part of the fundamental change that we are experiencing in the field of information work at the moment. For years we have had to keep collections of books and journals in case they proved useful. As they were produced in a paper format, distribution of them was costly and took a long time. Even now, with the fast transport systems we have available, it is expensive to obtain a copy of a city newspaper if that city is 6,000 or 12,000 miles away.

It was necessary to have stocks of information simply because it was so difficult to obtain. The Internet is quickly changing our perception of knowledge, in terms of its value and of its dissemination and storage. As long as I am able to obtain the information that I need within a couple of minutes by using the Internet, I have no need to store the same data on a bookshelf. Indeed, in many cases the information that is available electronically is going to be superior to the paper-based version. Not, of course, in terms of the facts themselves; the number of dead in the American Civil War does not change however I get the information, but if I obtain it electronically I may be able to import those statistics into a spreadsheet and look at them in any number of different ways. Moreover, electronic contents pages and indexes can be searched more quickly and effectively than their paper counterparts. There will always probably be a need to have some information available in a printed format, and I don't dispute that. However, I firmly believe that we need to move to a situation in which we look at a paper-based product and ask whether we can get rid of it, rather than where to shelve it.

An understandable worry at this point is that if we get rid of all of the books and the paper, are we not also very successfully doing ourselves out of our jobs? If you have already incorporated electronic access to information in your information service you will understand that this fear is quite unfounded. However, if you are considering embarking on this particular route, I'll go into some detail on how 'less is more' in this instance.

...and an intranet to gain!

Intranets deserve an entire book to themselves, so it is not really possible to do them justice here. However, they form an important part of the jigsaw of the emerging information centre, so I'll briefly explain what an intranet is before going on to talk about how it can be used.

An intranet is an organization's internal version of the Internet. Information can be stored on a central server, or can be distributed on machines around the organization as required. Information can be made available in HTML format (the same as that used when creating Web pages), and links can be made to data contained in other formats, such as word processed documents, spreadsheets or CD-ROM based databases. Consequently, the intranet forms an entire 'knowledge bank' for the organization. Information such as telephone lists, draft papers, discussion documents and so on can all be published on the intranet for people to access as and when necessary. If you're frowning at this point and saying 'yes, but isn't that just a description of the existing network we already have?', I should also make the point that existing networks require users to access a wide variety of different tools in order to obtain the information which is required, while an intranet works by providing that access under the umbrella of the Web browser.

Furthermore, organizations such as Dataware at

DID YOU KNOW?

Amazon.com listed over 80 different titles about intranets when I looked, and I am sure that will have doubled by now, so there are plenty to choose from!

http://www.dataware.com are providing systems to further integrate information into a single cohesive whole. Hypertext links between information increasingly enhance a system in which data can be 'mined', gathered from a variety of different sources and used to create new data sets. Of course, it is also possible to link to sites at other organizations, or to reach out to the rest of the Internet, creating an extranet.

The role of the information professional is central to the creation of a successful intranet; after all, we are talking about arranging and creating access to information albeit in a electronic, rather than paper based system. Who better to take on this role than those who spend their entire time doing just that in more traditional environments? The information professional is perfectly positioned to work with technical staff, the marketing department, public relations and so on to structure the information, choose and implement software solutions, train staff and publish information for themselves.

Far from having no work to do, a distributed system such as an intranet is going to mean a much more exciting life for the information professional of the future. There will be new technical skills to learn, such as HTML authoring, and a requirement to have a better understanding of how all these systems work. Perhaps more importantly than that, the professional is going to be drawn ever closer into a central key position in the organization; a 'just in time' approach means that future information requirements are going to have to be anticipated, resources identified, organized and published on the company intranet. Intelligent agents will be brought into service to a greater extent, because it will be impossible to keep up to date with all the information being published, but even when it has been located, someone will need to check the data for accuracy and authority. The information professional will be able to interrogate the intranet to find out what subjects people are interested in, what topics are of growing importance and which are of decreasing value to the organization.

DID YOU KNOW?

HTML stands for Hyper Text Markup Language, and is the code used to tell a browser how to display a Web page on the screen.

Commerce, the Internet and the information professional

In Chapter 6 I mentioned in passing the rise of commercial systems on the Internet, and how publishers are making use of it to increase their revenue streams. Methods of payment for the material that can be obtained are going to have an increasingly important effect on how we can all view and purchase material, and these will have considerable impact on future developments of both the Internet itself and the role of the information professional.

As we have seen, there are a variety of different commercial services available to the information professional and it should come as no surprise that there are a variety of methods of paying for the information required. The most obvious and widely used approach is to take out a subscription to a service in the same way that a CD-ROM subscription would be purchased – by contacting the company involved, ordering the service and paying the invoice. However, instead of receiving a series of discs you will be supplied with a user name and password. Other traditional methods of payment, by cheque or offline credit card transaction, are also widely used now and will be even more so in the future.

One payment method which I will go into a little detail over is that of micropayments. I have already alluded to this in Chapter 6 when talking about Northern Light, but I believe that it is going to become more common in the future. A micropayment system is a situation in which a company sells a product (very often an article) for a small sum of money, perhaps just a few pennies. While they do not make very much revenue from individual payments, the theory is that if enough people pay a small amount for a product the total revenue stream will be large. British Telecom has recently launched a payment service based on these lines, called BT Array, based at **http://www.btarray.bt.com**. At the time of writing, the test is still in a trial period, but appears to be working well. The principle behind the system is simple: users register with BT and provide credit-card details and their e-mail address over a secure server. They are then able to purchase products from any company (BT uses the term 'merchants') that has signed up with the scheme.

HINTS AND TIPS

If you intend to use commercial services and intend paying by credit card, please make sure that you are using a secure system to transfer your credit-card details – the Web site should state this up-front. If they do not, contact them before sending the information to confirm that your details will be encrypted so that no one else can read them. You may prefer to send your details by fax, phone or letter, but in the long run this may not be any safer! Do whatever you feel most comfortable doing.

BT keeps a running total of the purchases which have been made, and these will be charged to the user's credit card at regular intervals. Subscribers to the service will be able to check their account whenever they wish, check their purchases, and can settle their accounts early, if preferred.

At the moment there are only a few merchants who have signed up to the service, but one interesting example is the *Internet Magazine* at **http://www.internet-magazine. com/buy/** who are selling articles on Internet related matters at 75 pence each. BT are confident that this number will increase during the period of the trial and after the formal launch later in 1998.

The growth of commercial services on the Internet is having, and will continue to have, a profound effect on the way in which information professionals work. Before the rise of the Internet publishers sold information contained in discrete units – books or journals and a major part of the librarian's job was to provide easy access to this information by cataloguing and classifying these units. Even after CD-ROM technology was introduced, and publishers began to distribute larger amounts of information, it was still done using a physical form (in this case the optical disc) to arrange and ultimately control access to the information. Although superficially things had changed, information was still made available in physical units such as optical discs, and this artificial boundary meant that users had to subscribe to specific databases of information based on atoms (the optical discs) rather than digits (the electronic information).

However, it soon became clear that databases could be precached onto hard disk and publishers such as SilverPlatter ensured that their software could search across different databases. It was then only a short step to providing Internet access, as we have seen. It is now possible to allow users to access information in a completely different way; instead of having to choose individual databases to search, users can now ask for whatever information they require, regardless of artificial boundaries of database, book or journal. Online ordering direct to a user's mailbox has resulted in a situation in which the end-user can apparently bypass the information centre entirely. Superficially, therefore, it provides an all-too-realistic scenario in which the organization can dispense with the services of their information professionals!

You will be pleased to read, however, that I believe that the role of the information professional in the new commercially aware world of digital technology is going to be more valued, rather than less. What the end-user is accessing (and in many cases buying) is what I refer to as 'intermediate information', which only has value when it is used to produce an end result, such as a paper, a graph or a proposal. The value of this intermediate information will have been decided by the publisher or the author; they will have to make assumptions about who will want their information, how it can be used and how much the end result is going to be worth. A study of case law will be of particularly high value to a lawyer who needs the information in order to prepare a defence for a client, but the same information will have little or no value to a biologist, for example. Information professionals are going to be increasingly valued for their ability in finding the right sort of information at the right price, or less if possible!

The role is one that should not hold any horrors, since in many ways that is what the professional is doing at the moment; the big difference is in the medium used. Users will need much more training, guidance and assistance to get the best value out of the huge amounts of information which will be available, and will need to use systems that have been designed and implemented by information professionals working with technical staff. Information professionals therefore become facilitators, helping the end-users obtain information, rather than the gatekeepers they have been in the past.

We will also see other changes in the information industry as a result of this commercialization. In the past, publishers have been able to create revenue as a result of their control over copyright and the physical methods of publishing and distributing information. In the future, authors will be able to publish for themselves and use micropayment methods to obtain financial rewards for their labours. The obvious result of this is that we will see a huge explosion in personal publishing, with little or no control. Information professionals

DID YOU KNOW?

The Internet has created several millionaires, although none of them are information professionals as far as I know. If you want to find out who they are, visit http://www.pulver.com/ million/

are going to become increasingly involved with checking the authority of data, while the traditional publishers will need to encourage authors to continue to publish their work using them as the intermediary. Consequently they will have to provide value-added services in the way that BioMedNet is already doing (perhaps by drawing even more on the services of the information profession) and by adding that level of authority which will be missing from individual's publishing efforts. This will inevitably lead to a rise in new electronic publishers, and information professionals are going to be hard pressed to keep up with this and will spend much time checking the validity of different resources. This is already happening, as we saw when we looked at virtual libraries Chapter 7.

One final major change in approach is going to be the move from 'just in case' to 'just in time'. Paper based technologies meant that libraries had to keep large collections of information material just in case they were needed. Owing to the difficulties of transporting information in books and journals, it was simply not possible to locate, order and obtain information quickly enough, so vast collections of books and other resources such as newspapers and more recently videos needed to be kept for the few times in which the information contained in them was required. Electronically available data, coupled with low fees for access, means that it becomes much more feasible to maintain the processes and methods of data collection (the terminals, the intranets and so on) rather than maintaining the data itself. In this new environment the emphasis shifts towards being able to find the required data quickly and effectively, and possess it for a short period of time so that it can be referred to, manipulated and then disposed of. Of course, some information will have an ongoing use within an organization, and the information professional will be charged with obtaining it and putting it into databases where it can be retrieved on a regular basis using text retrieval or database management software in such a way that the end-user can access it easily.

Future developments

Five years ago very few people were aware of the Internet;

many of us still focused on optical technology as the best or most innovative way of making information available. Within half a decade the Internet has taken over, as more and more people use it, publish information on it and make their fortunes out of it. Every day new Web sites are created, new applications are launched and people discover new uses for the Internet. Consequently, it is a very brave person who would attempt to predict what will happen in this fast-changing environment. Perhaps the only certainty is that change will continue at frightening speed and the map will be constantly changing. The following section, however, attempts to do the impossible by alerting you to trends that you should be aware of so that you can keep a note of their development and make use of them as appropriate.

- The rise of intelligent agents. At the moment these are in their infancy; if you have tried out some of those mentioned in Chapter 8 this will come as no surprise at all. However, they will continue to improve and the level of sophistication will increase. Within a short space of time I expect them to become the preferred method of locating information for everything except the 'quick and dirty' search. Agents will be incorporated directly into intranets, and as they locate and retrieve information they will be able to import it directly into appropriate applications and will be able to alert staff to the existence of new data. The role of the information professional here will be to monitor the retrieved information and assess its value to the organization, to say nothing of being the individual who sets up the search profiles, updating them as necessary.
- Search engines will need to compete with agents, but I suspect that they will do this by incorporating them into the services they provide. We can already see search engines such as Yahoo! providing personalized pages, and this trend will continue. The search engines will be able to monitor the searches that are being run, learn from the sites which are retrieved from the results returned and will be able to run further searches automatically without prompting.

■ Micropayments will begin to reshape the whole publishing industry. Authors will be in a position to publish their work directly onto the Web and will be able to charge users small amounts of money every time their articles are retrieved, and as I discussed in Chapter 6 systems are already being put into place to facilitate this. Publishers will need to offset this loss of revenue by providing added-value services, perhaps by following the BioMedNet example, and will need to create communities of interest, links to new services and resources, and so on. As now, they will be in a good position to provide a level of authority to a publication by sending it for peer review. However, instead of this whole process taking months, faster communications will ensure that scientific and medical papers, for example, will be released much more quickly than at present.

■ Another implication leading on from this is that the traditional approach to scholarly publishing will dramatically change. University presses will need to evolve rapidly as less is published in paper formats and more electronically. Staff will need to reskill in order to take advantage of more flexible methods of publishing. Articles will increasingly include a rich array of multimedia resources, but, perhaps more importantly than that, they will be constantly changing. Printing in traditional formats fixes an article at its publication date, but in the future I see no reason why articles should not become almost like discussions in their own right. The peer review process will allow an author to change, alter and add to a document, and then electronically republish it. Others will then be able to comment on it, and the author will once again be able to change the article in the light of this. The danger here is that no one will keep archives of 'work in progress', so it will be necessary to establish systems that store earlier versions of a work in order to keep the historical perspective. Information professionals will, paradoxically, need to be as involved with the historical data as with the new.

■ Online journals will proliferate. Since it is cheaper to publish electronically, and easier to obtain a much wider circulation, we will see a rise in very specific titles. Information professionals are going to have to spend considerable time discovering these new titles (either manually or by use of agents) and will have to check their authority before alerting colleagues to their existence.

■ Virtual libraries will become increasingly valuable as professionals work together to locate, check and publish useful sources of constantly changing information. It will not take long before they outstrip the search engines in terms, of both usefulness and trust. A danger with search engines is that they mainly exist to generate revenue for their owners, and an obvious way of doing this will be to sell ranking positions, so that the company which pays the most will come at the top of a rankings list, regardless of how appropriate the content of its Web site is to the search which is being run. Virtual libraries, run for entirely different reasons, will not be in this position, and can provide true relevance and ranking services.

■ Push technology will continue to evolve. We looked briefly at the work that PointCast are doing in this area in Chapter 8; rather than waiting for you to go out and find information, push technology will simply stream data directly to the desktop or the intranet, working in conjunction with intelligent agents. As a consequence, information professionals are going to be bombarded with information as never before, and will need to install filter systems that will check the data and rank it for them into categories such as 'immediate', 'urgent', 'commercial advertisement' and so on. I can also foresee that systems will provide certain types of information at certain times of day, so that high-priority information which has been obtained throughout the night will be presented first thing in the morning, less urgent material an hour later, and football results at lunchtime!

■ Communication systems will also continue to improve. Mailing lists are very useful already, but they do not replace face to face contact. Video conferencing will become much easier, and groups of professionals will be able to meet on a more regular and convenient basis than is currently possible. Those individuals who still wish to speak directly to an information professional to explain their research topic and the type of information required will be able to do so, regardless of where they happen to be physically located. In a multinational organization research can continue twenty-four hours a day; if the information professional in London has to leave work at five o'clock he/she will be able to set up a video conference with a colleague in New York to pass on details of a search request and then go home, safe in the knowledge that the request is still being worked on. Next day a briefing might be waiting from a colleague in San Francisco who took the job on from New York. Rather than taking three days to obtain all the necessary information, it could be done apparently overnight.

■ If the concept of a 24 hour working day seems too horrific to contemplate, it will have benefits as well. Given powerful telecommunications, an increasing number of people will be able to work from home, and information workers will be close to the top of the queue. A multinational organization will be able to use its workforce more effectively, and if you decide to work an evening shift you can arrange with colleagues on another continent to take over their workload, enabling them to stop work early. As it will not be necessary to travel to work, people will be in a position to choose hours which suit them, rather than being dictated to by transport systems.

These are a few of the changes that I think we can expect to happen within the next five years, and indeed with most of them the basic structures are already in place, so I don't think that any of these ideas are too outlandish. Doubtless I've missed many important developments, but the problem with looking into the future is that it is possible to highlight so many different areas; if I had tried to be comprehensive I would have written a book twice the size!

Summary

In this chapter I've opened up some new avenues for you to explore for yourself, and provided some food for thought. If you have gained anything at all, I hope that it is an appreciation of the variety of resources and possibilities which the Internet provides to the information professional. We will continue to hone and refine our skills, and although we may not be using information in a physical format in the future, the role of the information professional has a long and exciting future ahead of it.

URLs mentioned in this chapter

http://www.dyslexiaonline.com/center.html
http://www.imdb.com
http://www.metaplus.com
http://www.dailywav.com/
http://sound-ring.com/index.html
http://www.mailbase.ac.uk
http://www.open.gov.uk
http://www.timeout.co.uk.
http://www.telegraph.co.uk
http://www.dataware.com
http://www.btarray.bt.com
http://www.internet-magazine.com/buy/
http://www.pulver.com/million/

11

Thirty tips and hints for better and quicker searching

Introduction

Understanding how search engines work, and what intelligent agents and gateways are, is only one of the skills a good Internet searcher requires. There are a number of other important points to be aware of in order to ensure that the time you spend on the Internet is fast and effective. This chapter is a miscellany of the tips and tricks that I've picked up in the time I've spent using the Internet. Some of them may do nothing more than save you a few keystrokes, while others may save you a lot of time.

Getting online and moving around the Web

1   Get the fastest Internet connection you can. If you are using a dial-up account to access the Internet, a modem running at 14,400 baud is the slowest you can really use, and you can expect to spend a lot of time twiddling your thumbs waiting for pages to download or for your e-mails to arrive in your mailbox. Think of your modem as a doorway: if it's a large doorway, you can get people (or data) going backwards and forwards with no problem. If it's a small doorway then people have to start forming orderly queues, and the whole thing slows down. Your modem is a little bit like that: the faster it is, the more data can go backwards and forwards. Consequently, it is worth investing in the fastest modem possible, and 33,300 baud or 56,000 baud will decrease the download time quite dramatically. A Web page which takes 50 seconds to download using a 14,400 modem will only take 27 seconds at 28,000 baud, or 19 seconds at 56,000. If your organization can afford the cost of a leased line run-

ning at 128,000 baud that same page will only take 6.8 seconds to appear on your screen. Of course, in actual practice you will need to consider that other factors, such as the time of day (mentioned in tip 2), will also affect the time it takes for the Web page to download onto your machine.

This is going to become increasingly important in the future as Web pages continue to evolve and include sound and moving image files as standard. You may already have noticed that some pages (usually those of corporates) are increasingly using multimedia, and without a fast connection you may just as well not bother to wait for the page to appear on your screen.

When and where it's best to search

2   This depends very much on where the site is that you're interested in going to. If, like me, you spend a lot of time using American sites, you'll find its best to search them either in the morning (up to about 12 o'clock) or later in the evening. This leaves the (morning their time) for the Americans to log on and get their news and mail, etc. Its surprising how much of a difference it makes! If you're one of my American readers, ignore this advice, and instead try UK sites during your afternoon, when we've all gone home for the day!

While the Internet doesn't really care about local/global issues, you may want to. Remember what the different time zones are; if you can get the same file or information from a site in the USA and from one in Australia, for example, my advice is to go to whichever country is currently 'asleep', since you'll get a faster response rate.

3   Searching for sites in your own country? Try and do it at odd hours; if you're awake, it's a fair bet that most of the rest of the UK is awake as well, and some of them will be trying to access the same sites as you. The more you can do first thing in the morning or late at night, the quicker it will all be.

Finding Web pages

4 The easiest way to find a Web page without using a search engine is to try and guess the URL of the site. It's certainly not an infallible method, but it is worth trying.

5 Become familiar with the major domain identifiers such as .com, .co.uk, .gov, ac.uk and country codes. Organizations will attempt to register memorable or easy to find addresses, so try a few possible combinations of name and domain identifiers. Naturally, if you do not find the correct site within a couple of attempts, you will have to fall back on the search engines, but the more you use the Web, the more likely you are to guess correctly.

6 Shorten the URL. We have all experienced this one — you find the perfect Web page with a search engine, and the summary looks perfect, but when you try to access it, it's not there any more. It may have been deleted, or it might just have been moved within the site. Shorten the URL one stage at a time and work your way back up the chain. Eventually you'll arrive at a page of some sort, which might give you an index to what else is on the site, and you might find the page you want listed at that point. For example, if the address you had was:

http://www.philb.com/search_engines/
publications/articles/freetext/altavista.htm
shorten it to:
http://www.philb.com/search_engines/
publications/articles/freetext/
then to:
http://www.philb.com/search_engines/
publications/articles/
and so on.

Finding information on a page

7 Once a page has loaded on the screen, you may have to spend some considerable time searching through it to find the keywords or phrases that you ran a search on, or you may simply wish to check a page to see if it contains the type of information that you are interested in. Don't scroll down through screen after screen both Netscape

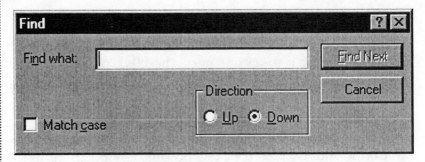

Fig. 11.1   *The Netscape Find box*

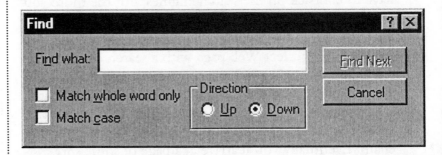

Fig. 11.1   *The Explorer Find box*

and Internet Explorer have features that allow you to find the required data. In Netscape, either choose 'Find in Page' from the Edit menu, or press Ctrl+F. This will bring up the dialog box shown in Figure 11.1. In Internet Explorer the command is the same and the dialog box is almost exactly the same, except for the option is to match the whole word only (see Figure 11.2). Both browsers also allow you to search again for subsequent occurrences. One word of warning here: you must wait for the entire page to load before using the Find option.

8   Do not forget to make use of the 'page up' and 'page down' keys! It is surprising how often people neglect their use. Some badly written Web pages will also load wider than the screen, which means that it is necessary to use the horizontal scroll bar to see everything on the page.

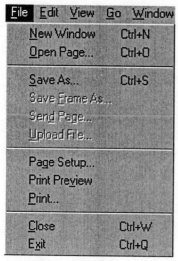

Fig. 11.3   *Netscape File menu options*

Saving pages

9 Once you have viewed the page on your screen, you may
wish to save it permanently. There are a number of possibilities here, depending on how you wish to save the data.
The easiest method is to use 'Save As' from the File
menu. Figure 11.3 displays Netscape's pull-down File
menu; Internet Explorer's File menu is virtually identical.

When you choose 'Save As' (or Ctrl+S), you will be
prompted to save the page as either a text or an HTML
file. If you intend to incorporate data from the page into
a word-processed document you should save it as a text
file, because saving it as an HTML file will also save all
the mark-up tags that were used to create the page. If you
wish to retain the formatting, you can save as HTML,
and then open the file in Word. However, if you wish to
view the page offline using your browser you must
choose the HTML option. Please be aware that if you
save a page in this way only the *text* will be saved, not the
graphics.

10 To save the graphics you should right-click on each
image and choose 'Save Image As' (Netscape) or 'Save
Picture As' (Internet Explorer). That will display another
dialog box prompting you to choose a file name and location. If you are intending to display the page using a

browser, my advice is to save both page and graphic images in the same folder. You will then need to edit the HTML code on the page, so that the tags which point to the images are directing your browser to look locally for the images, rather than at a remote file server. It is outside the remit of this title to go into detail about HTML code, so if you have doubts about this you are advised to talk to a colleague who has responsibility for writing Web pages and can sort out the tags for you. Alternatively in Chapter 12 you will find information about software packages which will save entire Web pages to disk for you, including graphics.

Printing pages

11 Alternatively, you may find it easier simply to print the Web page that you require. It should print out much the same as it appears on the screen, though you may find one or two differences in formatting, particularly if the Web page scrolls off the right-hand side of the screen.

   Sometimes you may print what appears to be an almost blank sheet of paper, which just shows the title and URL of the page. This usually happens when the Web page to be printed has light text on a dark background. The printer will not print a dark background (the waste of ink being astronomical!), but it will print the light coloured text in white, giving effectively a blank sheet. If this happens to you, the remedy is simple. You need to override the page colours to insert your own. In Netscape choosing, Edit/Preferences/Colors will display the dialog box shown in Figure 11.4. Set the text and background colours to black and white respectively, reload the page and then print it. In Internet Explorer you can choose View/Internet/Options to use a similar dialog box.

12 Alternatively, you could simply highlight the text you require, and copy and paste it into a word-processed document, although you will lose the page formatting this way.

Displaying pages

13 This is an obvious tip, but turn 'Automatically load

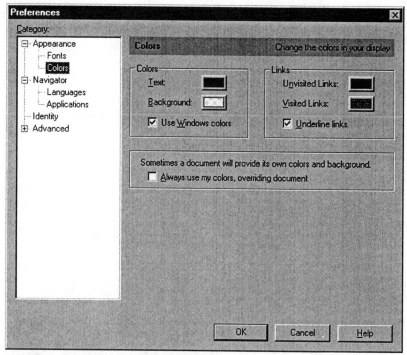

Fig. 11.4   *Netscape Color preferences*

images' off by using Edit/Preferences/Advanced in
Netscape or View/Internet/Options/Advanced in Internet
Explorer. This ensures that graphics are not loaded. A
good Web designer will ensure that alternative text is displayed in place of the graphic. If it isn't, you can try moving your cursor over the image and look in the bottom
left-hand corner of the browser screen; you might see a
new URL, which may give you some idea as to what will
happen if you click on the graphic (presuming of course
that it's a link, rather than a picture of the cat). If you
decide that you do want to see the images, you can turn
the 'load images' option back on again, and reload the
page.

Moving around the Web

14 If, like me, you get fed up with typing in the full address
of a Web page, it will come as a nice surprise to find out
that you don't always need to! In the Go to: box in
Netscape or Address box in Internet Explorer you can

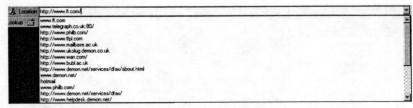

Fig. 11.5 *The Netscape option of showing recently visited sites*

generally get away without typing the **http://** and simply
type in the rest of the URL as in: **www.philb.com**. You
can, in some situations, reduce this even further – recent
versions of the browsers will accept **.com** as the default,
and will also make the assumption that the URL starts
with 'www', so you can actually reduce my URL to just
philb.

Returning to recently visited pages

15 There are a number of ways that you can use to return to
a page that you have recently visited. The most common
is to use the Back button on the browser, which will take
you back one page at a time in the sequence you viewed
them. This is fine if you simply wish to retrace one or
two steps, but is rather more annoying if you need to go
back several.

16 Take a look at the location or Go to: box at the top of the
Netscape and Internet Explorer browser screens, and particularly at the small down-arrow to the right-hand side.
Click on it, and you'll be presented with a list of recently
accessed sites, from which you can select the one you
want to revisit. This is not limited to the current session.
You can see this in operation in Figure 11.5.

17 You can also use a right-click on the current page; this
brings up a pop-up menu which allows you to move
backwards or forwards to other pages, which is quicker
than moving up to the Back option, although you'll still
be better off using the Go to: pull-down option if you
want to go back more than a few pages at once. You can
see this in Figure 11.6.

18 You can also see that this menu provides other functionality as well, allowing you to view information about the

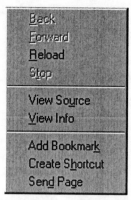

Fig. 11.6 *Pop-up menu in Netscape enabling you to move around the Web quicker*

page (View Source and View Info), add a bookmark, or send the page to a colleague, as well as other functions that are reasonably obvious.

Running more than one copy of the browser

19 Both Netscape and Internet Explorer provide you with the option of opening up a second copy of the browser, using Ctrl+N (for both browsers) or File/New/Window in Internet Explorer or File/New Window in Netscape. This allows you to keep two or more Web pages on the screen simultaneously, and is very useful in a number of situations. Quite often a page will take some time to download and display on the screen, and rather than sitting and twiddling your thumbs, opening another window allows you to begin to browse another page at the same site or to connect to another site and download a page from that as well. It may take slightly longer to download both pages this way, since the modem can only transmit a limited amount of data, but it can prove a fast and effective way to work in some situations.

20 Keep an eye on the Back button on your browser, because Web designers also make use of the 'open new window' function in the Web pages that they produce, and clicking on a link may sometimes open the target page in a new window, while keeping the old one open. In my opinion this is poor practice, since you are being deprived of the chance to decide for yourself whether to do this; and, more importantly, it is quite difficult to spot that it has occurred, particularly if the browser is being viewed in full screen. It is usually only when you try to use the Back button that you discover this has happened, since the new browser window you are using has nowhere to go back to. This can cause unnecessary confusion, particularly for novice users.

Bookmarks
Using bookmarks

21 Both Netscape and Internet Explorer allow you to create bookmarks or favorites, which are really just shortcuts to frequently accessed pages. Once you have discovered a valuable page, it is always worth bookmarking it – it can be quite frustrating trying to find a specific page the second time around without re-running a search or hunting through pages trying to find that elusive link! Creating a bookmark or favorite is straightforward – simply click on the Bookmarks/Add Bookmark option in Netscape, or Favorites/Add to Favorites option in Internet Explorer and the page will be added to the list.

22 When the browser adds the page to the list, it looks at the HTML title element on the page and uses that. If the title is sensible, such as 'Phil Bradley's Home Page', you will probably remember exactly why the page was bookmarked, but if the title is something less informative, such as 'My Home Page', it will be necessary either to go back to the page in order to jog your memory or to edit the title yourself to something more sensible. I'll cover just how that is done in a moment.

23 Give serious thought to deciding on the best way to arrange your bookmarks as early as possible, to limit the amount of sorting that has to be done in the future. Once you start adding Web pages to your bookmarks, before long you will have created a list that covers several hundred sites, making the process of finding a specific page quite difficult. A sensible list of folders and subfolders will avoid the mess and confusion that results from a single list. Both Netscape and Internet Explorer provide options to arrange the bookmarks into a hierarchical structure

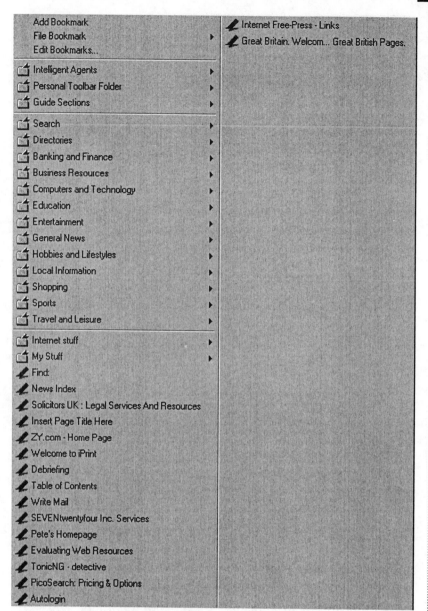

Fig. 11.7   Netscape bookmarks

very similar in principle to the method used by Yahoo! to arrange information, so you are basically creating your own index to the Internet. Netscape comes with a number of bookmarks pre-set in categories, as can be seen in Figure 11.7 with some of my own.

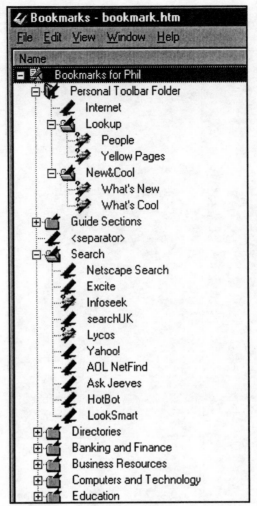

Fig. 11.8 *Editing Netscape bookmarks*

Editing bookmarks

24 If you choose to add more bookmarks, by default they will
simply appear in a chronological list in the folder 'My
Stuff'. A more sensible way to use the power of bookmarking is to add a new bookmark and then use the Edit feature
to move it either to a pre-existing folder, or to a new folder
created from scratch. This will bring up a new dialog box
that looks something like that seen in Figure 11.8.

Clicking on File/New Folder allows you to add a new
folder to the bookmark list, and then it becomes a simple
operation to click and drag bookmarked pages into the

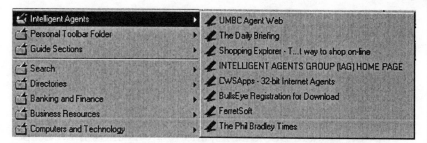

Fig. 11.9 *A new Netscape bookmarks folder – Intelligent Agents*

new folder. Figure 11.9 shows the same list as found in Figure 11.8, but with the addition of a new folder called Intelligent Agents. The name of any folder or bookmark title can be changed by going to the Edit menu, choosing Bookmark Properties, and entering a more suitable name for the item. Although I have chosen Netscape Navigator here, Internet Explorer has the same functionality within its Favorites menu. If you choose Favorites/Organize Favorites, Internet Explorer displays a dialog box similar to Figure 11.10, and you can then add, delete, move and

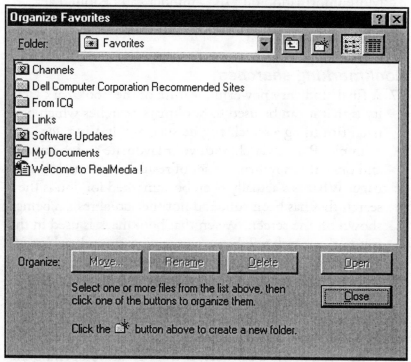

Fig. 11.10 *Organizing Favorites with Internet Explorer*

rename shortcuts to personalize the list in the same way
as can be done with Netscape.

Updating bookmarks

25 Netscape also has a very useful feature allowing you to
update your bookmarks regularly. The View menu has an
option Update Bookmarks, and if this is chosen Netscape
will visit each bookmarked page in turn to see if it has
been updated since you last visited it. This is done
quickly and effectively, and a little icon displayed next to
each page that has changed. This of course means that it
is not necessary to go and visit each page manually, since
the browser will do this more quickly itself. Internet
Explorer has its own, rather more complex, updating
facility called Subscriptions.

26 Alternatively, there is a Web-based utility called URL-
minder that keeps a track of the Web pages you are interested in and sends you an e-mail when they change. It's a
perfect resource for monitoring URLs on your behalf.
More information on URL-minder can be found at:
**http://www.netmind.com/URL-minder/
URL-minder.html**

Bookmarking searches

27 A final, and very powerful, feature of the bookmark facility is that it can be used to bookmark searches which have
been run using a search engine such as AltaVista, for
example. Run a search with your favourite search engine,
and once it has returned a set of results, bookmark that
page. What has actually been bookmarked for you is the
search that has been run, and not the actual results being
shown on the screen. When that bookmark is used in the
future the search will be re-run, giving an updated list of
Web pages. This can be helpful if used in conjunction
with a date limit, since it means that it is easy to create a
current awareness service.

Choose a new home page

28 When you install a browser, it will default to opening the
home page of the company that created it. While there is

useful information to be found at the homes of both Netscape and Microsoft, you will probably find in a short space of time that your first port of call is a search engine, or perhaps the home page of your own organization. Rather than bookmarking it, you can tell the browser that it should load that page as its home page. Both browsers that I use always start by loading AltaVista, for example, since I usually go onto the Web to look for something, and that is my preferred search engine.

To change the home page in Netscape choose Edit/ Preferences/Navigator/Home page, and in Internet Explorer choose View/Internet Options/General/Home page, and simply type in the new URL that you wish to make your home page. If you wish, you can also tell the browser to open your home page automatically at start up.

29 Alternatively, there is no reason why you should not create your own home page, writing HTML code to set links to useful pages, different search engines or virtual libraries for example. Once you have done this, you can simply tell the browser to look locally on your hard disk to find the new home page, using the method just described. If you wish to do this, but are not confident in writing HTML pages yourself, you could copy the HTML code that I have included as Appendix 1 and save the file onto your hard disk, and point your browser to that. It should look very much like the screenshot in Figure 11.11. A new home page, listing useful search engines, created in a matter of moments!

A more extensive version, including more search engines, can be found at my Web site at **http://www. philb.com/** and you are welcome to copy and edit the page for your own needs.

Getting more out of your browser's cache

30 Understand your browser's cache. When your browser visits a page, it copies the information (both the text and the graphics) back onto your own computer and displays the page on the screen. It does this by storing the information in a cache, in memory or as temporary files on

Search Engines Starter Page.

The search engines listed below will help you find what you are looking for on the Internet.

General Search Engines	Name of the Search Engine
Free text search engines	Alta Vista
	HotBot
	Lycos
	Northernlight
Index based search engines	Excite
	Metaplus
	Yahoo
Multi-search engines	Internet Sleuth
	Inference find
Yellow and White pages	Biographies
	Electronic Yellow Pages
	FOUR11
	Who's Who Online
Searching for political/country information	CIA World Factbook
	EuroFerret
	European Maps
	British Government

Fig. 11.11 *A search engine home page*

the hard disk. When you ask to view a page that you have recently looked at, the browser is intelligent enough to retrieve it from its cache, rather than going back to the original server and obtaining the information all over again. That is why you will generally find that pages you have recently visited will appear on your screen virtually instantaneously.

Both Netscape and Internet Explorer provide you with options to increase the size of your cache, which means that more pages can be stored; if the cache is small, the browsers are constantly overwriting old pages with new ones, increasing the chance that they will have to revisit sites. The larger the cache, the less this will happen.

In Netscape click on Edit/Preferences and then click on the '+' sign to the left of the Advanced options, and you should then see the dialog shown in Figure 11.12 This will then allow you to increase both the disk and the memory cache. The sizes you can increase them to depend on the configuration of your computer, and the amount of hard disk space and memory it has available. If

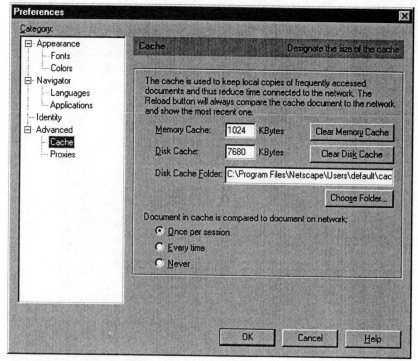

Fig. 11.12 *Configuring Netscape's cache*

you have any doubts you should contact your technical support staff.

In Internet Explorer it is necessary to choose View/ Internet Options/General/Temporary Internet files/ Settings, at which point you should see a dialog box similar to that shown in Figure 11.13. Simply slide the bar across to the right; the further you move it, the more space will be assigned to the cache. Once again, if you are in any doubt, contact your technical support staff.

Summary

■ Even shortcuts which just save you a keystroke or two are worth using, because they will cumulatively save you a lot of time.

■ Be flexible in your approach to searching, particularly the time of day that you search.

■ Try guessing now and then – you never know, it may work!

■ Learn your browser inside out. There are lots of little

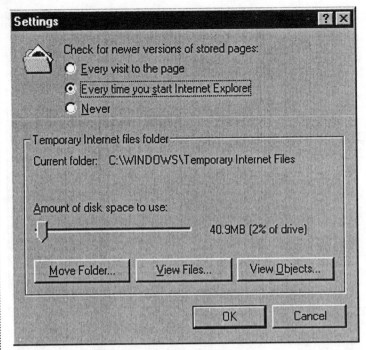

Fig. 11.13   *Changing Internet Explorer's cache*

tricks that you can use that will improve its performance and effectiveness, which means that *your* performance and effectiveness will be improved.

URLs listed in this chapter

http://www.netmind.com/URL–minder/
        URL–minder.html
http://www.philb.com/

12

Sources for further help and assistance

Introduction

One of the major characteristics of the Internet, as I'm sure you are aware, is that it is constantly changing and developing. It is therefore an extraordinarily difficult task to keep up with new search engines, changes in existing ones (AltaVista has changed its search engine interface twice while I have been writing this book), new versions of software, new packages, new sites, increased coverage for different subjects, new mailing lists and newsgroups, to mention just a few. Not only are the resources themselves proliferating quickly, but, as you can see, the list of things to keep a watch on is almost endless as well!

In this chapter I want to bring to your attention a variety of resources which can help you keep on top of what is happening within the world of the Internet; if you can spend just half an hour a week checking them, you should stay abreast of key changes and advances. Moreover, if you need to obtain a quick overview of a particular subject area many of the resources that I mention provide useful briefings that cover the major points.

General information resources
Search Engine Watch
http://www.searchenginewatch.com
This site is maintained by Danny Sullivan, who is well known within the industry for providing current and practical information, and his site reflects this. Search Engine Watch is a resource that I use weekly, if not more often. It is divided into several sections:

- **Guide to search engines**. This section is written primarily for Web page designers and developers, but provides an interesting sidelight for users of search engines.
- **Search engine facts and fun**. If you require a brief overview of the different search engines, this is a concise description of them, with their advantages and disadvantages.
- **Search engine status report**. Here you will find statistics on how well the search engines are doing, how many pages they index, how current they are, and so on.
- **Search engine resources**. A collection of reviews, tutorials, copyright information, and a glossary of search engine terms, can be found here.
- **Search engine report**. Danny provides a monthly e-mail newsletter on the latest happenings relating to search engines. This is a free service, and only takes a few moments to skim through. It is always full of useful information of interest to people who search the Internet regularly.

Although the site is free, there is a subscription service available for $25 per year. Subscribers can obtain exclusive content which is not available on the free pages, more information than is contained in the free reports, in-depth fact files and access to research that Danny is working on.

Web Reference
http://webreference.com/
As the name suggests, this site is a good resource that can be used to jump off into different aspects of the Internet. Some of the subjects covered are:

- **Design issues**. While the design of Web sites might not at first glance be of much direct value to searchers, it is a good way of keeping up with new developments and software, and can provide pointers on what new packages you should consider obtaining.
- **E-Commerce**. This section provides many links to discussion documents and sites that are involved in this growing area of importance.

■ **Roadmap**. This is a 27-lesson Internet training workshop which has been made available free of charge. I doubt that experienced users would learn much of value, but it is a resource that novice users could be directed towards for some initial training.

■ **Interviews**. This section provides readers with an opportunity to hear what a variety of Internet experts think about different subjects.

■ **Resources**. Links to information on search engines, new software, HTML coding, intranets and so on.

Trade Shows
http://events.internet.com

The Internet Conference Calendar
http://www.conferences.calendar.com

If you want to find out which exhibitions, trade shows, symposia, workshops or seminars are coming to your city, these sites are a useful resource to find out exactly that.

Browserwatch
http://www.browserwatch.internet.com

This is another site which is worth bookmarking. It describes itself as the 'leading site for information on browsers and plug-ins'. The site provides information on the current state of play of the different browsers and how to get the best out of them, and gives a list of links to enable you to download the latest plug-in software.

Internet News
http://www.InternetNews.com/

Another useful site to keep yourself up to date with new developments in the industry. It has separate sections on:

■ browsers
■ deals, co-ventures and partnerships
■ an Internet advertising report
■ Internet stocks report
■ international news relating to the Internet
■ business and commercial news
■ new products

- intranet news
- information on Internet service providers.

CNET
http://www.cnet.com
ZDnet
http://www.zdnet.com
Both of these sites provide more general information on computers and computing, but also have significant information specifically relating to the Internet. They contain new and breaking stories, articles on many different aspects of the Internet, statistical information and briefings. ZDnet also offers what it calls the ZDnet University at **http://www. zdu.com** which is a commercial service offering a variety of different online training courses, some relating to the Internet.

The December List
http://www.december.com/cmc/info/
This site, maintained by John December, has a wealth of information regarding online communications and the Internet. It is a comprehensive collection for both trainers and students, providing access to organizations, forums, articles, and bibliographies.

Internet service providers
http://thelist.internet.com/
Access providers
http://www.thedirectory.org/
If you ever need to find out information on service providers, these sites link to over 10,000 of them.

Internet hoaxes
http://ciac.llnl.gov/ciac/CIACHoaxes.html
Never a week goes by when I am not informed by e-mail of some new virus which is going to destroy my computer. A virus warning should be taken seriously, of course, but the first place to check is this site, maintained by the US Department of Energy. The Computer Incident Advisory Capability (CIAC) monitors virus warnings and keeps a list

of hoaxes. Please check out the warning first, before sending it onto colleagues.

The Netiquette Home Page
http://www.fau.edu/rinaldi/netiquette.html

As I mentioned in Chapter 9, there are certain things that you should and should not do, when posting to newsgroups and mailing lists. This site tells you everything that you need to know about how to be polite in your dealings with other people on the Internet.

Glossary of Internet terms
http://www.matisse.net/files/glossary.html

If you've ever wondered what some of those strange little TLAs (three-letter acronyms) mean, this is a good place to find out. This site will also provide you with information on four- and five-letter acronyms as well!

Mailing lists

As you'll have learned from Chapter 9, mailing lists can be a very useful way of keeping up to date with what is happening in various subject areas. I find out a lot of information about the Internet, search engines, new sites and so on simply because someone has been kind enough to post to an appropriate list with details, and I try to do the same in return.

I checked some of the resources that I mentioned in that chapter in order to find suitable mailing lists, and a list of some of them is included below.

Mailbase lists
http://www.mailbase.ac.uk

- **lis–pub–libs**: This list covers issues arising from implementing the Internet in a public library.
- **lis–ukolug**: UKOLUG is a leading UK group for online, CD-ROM and Internet searchers, and contains lots of useful hints, tips and pointers to a variety of different resources.
- **pin**: Policing the Net. Issues covered in this mailing list focus on the ethical, moral and political responsibilities of the Internet.

- **sci-ed-inet**: Research into the use of the Internet for scientific education in the UK.
- **web-research-uk**: This mailing list covers UK-specific issues and announcements dealing with Internet research on the Web.

These are just a small number of the mailing lists that specifically cover the Internet, and joining instructions and further details on all of the above lists can be obtained directly from Mailbase.

Liszt
http://www.liszt.com

- **net-happenings**: This is quite a busy list, since it provides information on new sites, events, publications and training, but it is worthwhile subscribing to.
- **tourbus**: This list provides a 'virtual tour of cyberspace'; it is useful for novice users, and answers many of the questions that they have regarding the Internet.

Detailed instructions on joining the lists can be found at Liszt itself.

Spam

I mentioned spam in passing in Chapter 9; if you recall, it is the Internet equivalent of 'junk mail'. This is sometimes posted directly to newsgroups and mailing lists, but you may unfortunately also find it turning up in your e-mail box. If your e-mail address is on a Web page, if you post to newsgroups and visit Web sites, or if your e-mail address is to be found in people servers, there is a strong probability that you will end up on various spammers' lists and will be sent unsolicited e-mail. I generally receive five or six such e-mails per day, offering me the chance to get rich quickly, make money selling products from my Web site, launder money, have dubious conversations with scantily clad women, or various other illegal methods of making money. This last type is usually known as scamspam. I have heard of colleagues who get the same e-mails, up to thirty or forty a day. Even if you do not read them, it still takes time to delete them from your mailbox, and to add insult to injury you are paying download charges for the privilege!

It is tempting to write back to these people, particularly those who offer to take you off their lists, but please be wary. Replying just indicates that the spammer has found a valid e-mail address, and you may simply end up on other lists, increasing the amount of unwanted mail that you receive. Many spammers will forge their e-mail addresses anyway, so you have no way of responding to them, or worse, you'll send an irate response to an innocent individual whose name has been misappropriated by these unscrupulous people.

There are a number of Web sites that provide you with further information, assistance and detailed technical advice on how to combat this particular menace.

Help stop scam spammers
http://www.junkemail.org/scamspam/
This site provides background to spam: lawsuits, legislation, site listings, tips on spotting scams, and the opportunity to report any scams that are sent to you.

The Federal Trade Commission
http://www.ftc.gov
The FTC site is working for consumer protection, and provides legal advice and guidance as well as other detailed information on current scams.

SPAM-L FAQ
http://oasis.ot.com/~dmuth/spam-l
This document is the Frequently Asked Questions from the spam mailing list, which is a mailing list for the discussion of the subject, rather than a list used by spammers! As well as good introductory information, it goes into great detail on how to spot spammers, decipher e-mail message headers, and report spam that you receive.

Fight spam on the Internet
http://spam.abuse.net/
This is a useful introductory guide to the subject, covering areas such as 'What is spam?', 'Why is it bad?', 'What to do',

'What not to do'.

ZDnet articles
**http://www4.zdnet.com/anchordesk/story/
story_index_19970819.html**

ZDnet writers have produced a series of articles on spam, and also provide technical details on how to set-up e-mail filters to reduce the amount that you get.

Junkmail
http://www.csn.net/~felbel/jnkmail.html

This is a private site, run by an individual who is keen to stop spam. As well as material similar to that already mentioned, there are useful links to other resources, guidelines on what to do, hints and tips, newsgroup lists, discussions of privacy issues and summaries of anti-spam legislation.

Using search engines

There are probably more resources that cover this particular subject area than any other, and I suspect that I could have written an entire book just listing and annotating them. I have gathered together a list of those which I have consistently found most useful myself.

Reviews of search engines collected by Sheila Webber
http://www.dis.strath.ac.uk/business/search.html

Sheila has created a very useful and constantly updated list of links to articles and sites that review search engines, provide descriptions of engines, and discuss search strategies.

Web search tool features
http://www.unn.ac.uk/features.htm

Ian Winship maintains a regularly updated list of features and techniques for using the common search engines. It provides a useful short summary of what it is and is not possible to do with search engines, in a clear and easy to use format.

Search Engine Showdown
http://imt.net/~notess/search/index.html

Greg Notess has established a site which provides summaries, reviews and descriptions of the major search engines, together with links to articles on search strategies, subject directories, multisearch engines, statistics and news.

The Spider's Apprentice
http://www.monash.com/spidap.html
Monash Information Services have put together a site which links the viewer to a great many different resources such as:

- how to use search engines
- a discussion of search engines
- what's new in the world of search engines
- tips on smarter searching
- how search engines work
- an analysis of popular search engines
- a current list of the biggest, most comprehensive, usable, relevant and useful search engines.

Understanding and comparing Web search tools
http://www.hamline.edu/library/bush/handouts/
    comparisons.html
The Bush library at Hamline University has created a page of links to about 20 high quality articles which go into great detail on many different aspects of search engines.

Phil Bradley's Web site
http://www.philb.com
Modesty forbids me from saying too much about my own site, but I do have a variety of resources available, for novice and advanced searchers on search engines of all types and reviews of a number of them.

Search secrets mailing list
http://www.search-secrets.com/
This site provides details on how to join this particular mailing list, which claims to ensure that you will 'learn the latest search engine secrets, technology, tips, tricks, suggestions and pointers!'.

What's new services

It is difficult keeping up to date with what is happening on the Internet: which new resources have gone online, new Web sites, new mailing lists and so on. When people find new and useful resources they often post details in appropriate newsgroups or mailing lists, but a number of Web sites also exist just to publish information of this nature. Inevitably, since the lists are usually chronological, focusing on new sites on a day-to-day basis, they are almost random collections, but they can prove to be a useful resource if there is a global event, for example. At the time of writing the World Cup is being played, with many new sites being made available every day, so the what's new services act almost like a current awareness service.

Internet Week
http://techweb.cmp.com/internetwk/
Internet Week is an electronic newspaper that provides information on today's news, trends, reviews, resources, awards, an events calendar, articles and highlights.

What's new too!
http://newtoo.manifest.com/page1.html
This is a straightforward listing of new sites that have been submitted to the site. It has little internal arrangement, but is worth browsing if you have the time.

Yahoo! news
http://biz.yahoo.com/news/internet.html
Each day Yahoo! collects all the news stories (generally 30–40 per day) that they have found which relate to the Internet. This site tends to focus on the media and press releases rather than on new sites, and is therefore useful if you need to keep up with Internet business trends.

What's new from www.announce
http://www.cs.rochester.edu/u/ferguson/
     announce.www/
A useful newsgroup is **comp.info.systems.www.announce**, to which people can post details of new and updated sites and

other related information. This Web site acts as an archive of the newsgroup, with an index of articles for today, this week, this month and previous months.

Netscape's what's new

http://netscape.yahoo.com/guide/whats_new.html

Netscape and Yahoo have combined to create a general guide to what is new on the Internet, with various categories such as new Web sites, archives, category of the day and daily entertainment.

The Scout report

http://wwwscout.cs.wisc.edu/scout/report

The Internet Scout Project comes from the Computer Sciences Department at the University of Wisconsin, and is a weekly publication of interest to researchers and educators, being described by the department as a 'fast convenient way to stay informed of valuable resources on the Internet'.

What's new

http://www.whatsnew.com/whatsnew/

This is another site which provides listings of new Web sites, with specific versions for the UK, US and Europe, as well as recommended sites and the editor's choice.

Bibliographies and bookshops

If you are the type of reader who skims through a book, you will already have noticed that I have not included a bibliography or further reading list. There are several reasons for this: there are already far too many titles available to allow me to be comprehensive; any bibliography would be out of date before it was printed; and it is easier to obtain your own using Internet bookshops.

Internet bookshops exist in large numbers, and Yahoo! alone lists over 300 of them. I have listed below three of the ones that I use regularly, and it is only a few moment's work to produce a bibliography specific to your own particular needs.

Amazon
http://www.amazon.com

Amazon boasts over 3 million titles available, and is probably the best known of all the Internet bookshops. It provides customer reviews and author interviews and allows you to search by keyword or subject. The information returned for each title is basic, and the search features are limited, but on the other hand it is a very comprehensive service. Amazon also offers another service called Eyes, which is an automated searcher, tracking every newly released book; it will send you an e-mail when a title is published that matches your interests.

Blackwell Bookshop
http://bookshop.blackwell.co.uk

This site allows you to search by author or title, and the results returned provide full bibliographical details, plus a description and contents list.

The Internet Bookshop
http://www.bookshop.co.uk

The Internet Bookshop provides similar services to the other two, allowing you to search for author, title, ISBN, publisher or series. The Internet Bookshop equivalent of Eyes is 'Jenny, your personal librarian'.

Software

The Internet has always thrived on diversity and variety; there is never only one way of doing something, and usually there are several. This is certainly the case with software: if one organization produces a utility to perform a particular function it will not take long before three more do exactly the same thing.

In this section I look at some of the different types of utility that are available, together with why you might consider using them. This is not in any way a complete listing, but should simply be regarded as an overview of some of the available packages. I have not given prices, since these change quite quickly, and many of the products available are either freeware, which means that they can be used for as long as you wish without payment, or shareware, which means that they should be registered and paid for at the end of the trial period. Further details can be obtained from the company making the product available in each case.

Although there are many different software libraries available on the Internet, the only resource that I have ever needed to use is the Tucows site at **http://www.tucows.com**. It has over 400 mirror sites around the world, which means that it should not be difficult to find a site close to your own location in order to speed up downloads. Currently there are over 1,000 programs available for download, and Tucows has a good 'What's Moo' section, listing newly available software.

Browsers

The two major browsers are of course those produced by Netscape and Microsoft. The advantage of using either of these is that they are easily available (often from the free CD-ROM discs found on the covers of computer magazines) and Web authors write and design Web sites that utilize their functionality to the full. However, they do have their disadvantages as well, in that both of them are large and will quite happily consume several megabytes of hard-disk space, even on a minimal installation. Although these two are generally the default choice for a Web browser, there are over a dozen other browsers that may be more appropriate or effective for you to use.

■ Opera: **http://operasoftware.com**
Opera is a good browser to use by people who only have access to older computers, such as 386-based machines, or those who are visually challenged, since it is very easy to change the display of the Web page on the screen, particularly with regard to font size.

■ Surfin' Annette: **http://www.spycatcher.com**
This browser is useful if you are likely to have children searching the Internet, or if you decide to make your machines available for public access, but do not wish to run the risk of users looking at objectionable material. It utilizes various levels of protection, and can block access by site or by words contained on the Web page.

Bookmark utilities

As we have already seen in Chapter 11, the bookmarks that can be created using Netscape or Internet Explorer are very useful indeed, and if used correctly can become your own index to the Internet. If you upgrade to a new version of the same browser, it will be intelligent enough to use your existing bookmarks, but a problem can occur if you decide to switch between browsers. Luckily, however, there are a large number of utilities which can convert Netscape bookmarks into Internet Explorer favorites and vice versa. Others will even take your bookmarks and create an HTML page from them, which could then become your start page when searching the Internet.

■ Bookmark Converter: **http://www.abc.se/~m9761/ bm_conv**
Simply converts bookmarks between different versions of Netscape and Internet Explorer.

■ Bookmark Wizard: **http://www.moonsoftware.ee**
This utility will create an HTML page of your bookmarks, as well as converting them between the two main browsers.

Offline browsers

An offline browser will allow you to specify a particular site that you want to browse, and it will then go online and 'collect' the pages for you, download them to your hard disk, and log off. You can then view the site offline, thereby saving connect charges. Such a browser can be very useful if you need to spend a lot of time looking at a single large site, particularly if navigation around the site is not as clear as perhaps it should be.

■ Go Ahead Got It!
http://www.goahead.com/gotit/index.htm
This utility is slightly unusual, in that as well as saving pages to disk for you to view later, it attempts to predict which page(s) you will visit next on a site and downloads them in advance. Consequently, when you decide to move to another page, it has already been downloaded in

the background, bringing the page up immediately for you to view.

■ WebWhacker **http://www.ffg.com/whacker/**
WebWhacker was one of the first offline browsers, and it is simple to install and use, downloading either single pages or an entire site for you to view later at your leisure.

Cache viewers

As we have already seen, browsers will store recently visited pages in a cache. They can then be quickly retrieved by the browser and displayed on the screen; the browser does not need to go back to the Web site to obtain the same data again. If you are offline and wish to view your cache, these utilities will re-create the pages for you quickly. Internet Explorer in offline mode will allow you to view pages for the 'History' window, loading them from the cache if they are available. If they are no longer in the cache it will offer to go online and retrieve them. This is slightly different from an offline browser, in that a cache viewer can only display pages that you have visited, rather than pages you have told the offline browser to go and collect for you.

■ UnMozify for Netscape
http://www.evolve.co.uk/unmozify
■ UnMozify for Internet Explorer
http://www.evolve.co.uk/unmozify
These products, produced by the same company allow you to retrieve pages in both the Netscape and Internet Explorer caches.

Multimedia applications

The Web might have been just text a very long time ago, but now it is a riot of still images, sound and moving images. Browsers are able to cope with some of these different media without a problem – they can all display images, for example. However, an increasing number of Web sites are utilizing other forms of data, which browsers cannot cope with themselves. Many utilities exist which can be called upon by the browser to display this data in the appropriate format. Once they have been downloaded, the installation usually includes a method of linking them to the browser you are using so that the process of displaying data held in different media formats is done automatically with no further work on your part.

A good Web page will inform you that you are about to view information in a multimedia format and will offer you the opportunity to go to an appropriate Web site to download the necessary application, so you may prefer simply to wait until you have a need to do this. On the other hand, it may save you time if you can spend an afternoon downloading some of these utilities beforehand, rather than having to waste time installing the utility in order to view something which is urgently required.

■ Real Player: **http://www.real.com**
   Real Player will automatically play sound files and display moving images on your screen, and can also be configured to connect to Internet radio stations to provide a live feed.
■ Acrobat Reader: **http://www.adobe.com**
   Acrobat PDF files are sometimes created by organizations or individuals who want to retain the original 'look and feel' of a paper document, rather than change it into a HTML file. In order to view a PDF file, it is necessary to install a plug-in utility which can read it and then display it in your browser window.
■ QuickTime Player: **http://quicktime.apple.com/**
   QuickTime Player will play moving images (with soundtrack) from almost any movie format.

Anti-virus protection

Sensible users will always be alert to the danger of downloading a file containing a virus, but will not become so paranoid that they stop using the Internet completely. It is certainly possible to download a virus, usually embedded in another program or document file, but in my experience it is highly unlikely. The greatest friend of a virus is anonymity, and most viruses are passed from machine to machine by individuals using floppy disks to transfer files, without checking either the files or the floppy disk.

This is unlikely to happen on the Internet, because you are making a specific choice to copy a file, and will in all probability remember where you got it from. If it later transpires that the file contained a virus it should not be difficult to trace it back to the source. Furthermore, any reputable site will check regularly to ensure that their files do not contain a virus of any sort. In the years that I have been using the Internet I have only discovered one instance of a virus being maliciously transmitted; given the number of files available and number of people downloading them, this is a remarkably small figure!

It is possible to pass on a virus using e-mail attachments. For example, a Word document may contain a macro virus designed to harm your system. If you receive any such attachment from someone that you do not know, I would suggest that, before opening it, you write back to them and ask them who they are and why they have sent you the file. In fact, even if you do know the person who sent you the attachment they may have unwittingly distributed the virus to you; knowing your source is not necessarily a guarantee, so please do check!

It is also always sensible to backup your hard disk on a regular basis, depending on how valuable your information is. Suggestions range from once a day to once a week, but you should seek advice from your technical-support department on this point. It is also sensible to have effective virus protection software on your machine, and I have given four examples of good utilities below. However, once again you should talk to your technical-support department, since they may already have installed such software on machines within your organization.

■ Norton AntiVirus
http://www.symantec.co.uk/region/uk/product/navbrochure/
The Norton suite is on of the best known packages, used by over 15 million people worldwide. The software provides comprehensive antivirus protection at every possible entrypoint and subscribers can also obtain monthly downloads of new information.

■ Dr Solomon: **http://www.drsolomon.com**
Dr Solomon's provides a wide number of different virus protection packages for work, groupware, servers, home use and for use on the Macintosh. Subscribers can obtain updates to their software directly over the Internet.

■ McAfee ViruScan: **http://www.mcafee.com/**
This product is well known and powerful, including background and on-demand scanning. Updates are available from the site to catch new virus programs that have been created.

■ ViruSafe95: **http://www.eliashim.com**
This product offers online protection when downloading files from Web pages, allowing you to obtain files without the danger of downloading a virus with them.

Organizations

Most, if not all, library and information science groups are now heavily involved in the Internet, by providing publications and training courses or by funding research. It is always worth contacting your local organizations to see what work they are doing in this field. Some national and international organizations' Web pages are given below:

■ The American Library Association: **http://www.ala.org**
■ Aslib: **http://www.aslib.co.uk**
■ The Canadian Library Association: **http://www.cla.amlibs.ca**
■ International Federation of Library Associations and Institutions: **http://www.ifla.org**
■ The Library Association: **http://www.la-hq.org.uk**
■ TFPL: **http://www.tfpl.com**.

Magazines and journals

Many magazines related to the Internet are now published throughout the world, and these can provide very useful sources of information: new developments, new sites, 'how to' articles, information on software and so on. Yahoo! provides a useful listing of them at **http://www.yahoo.com/Computers_and_Internet/Internet/Magazines**.

Summary

In this chapter I have provided links to a number of resources which can assist you in further explorations of the Internet, as well as details of software that you can download and install to make your searching more effective. These Web pages are worth visiting and bookmarking, since they make the whole process of keeping up to date with developments so much easier.

URLs mentioned in this chapter

http://www.searchenginewatch.com
http://webreference.com/
http://events.internet.com
http://www.conferences.calendar.com
http://www.browserwatch.internet.com
http://www.internetnews.com/
http://www.cnet.com
http://www.zdnet.com
http://www.zdu.com
http://www.december.com/cmc/info/
http://thelist.internet.com/
http://www.thedirectory.org/
http://ciac.llnl.gov/ciac/CIACHoaxes.html
http://www.fau.edu/rinaldi/netiquette.html
http://www.matisse.net/files/glossary.html
http://www.mailbase.ac.uk
http://www.liszt.com
http://www.junkemail.org/scamspam/
http://www.ftc.gov
http://oasis.ot.com/~dmuth/spam-l
http://spam.abuse.net/
http://www4.zdnet.com/anchordesk/story/
    story_index_19970819.html
http://www.csn.net/~felbel/jnkmail.html
http://www.dis.strath.ac.uk/business/search.html
http://www.unn.ac.uk/features.htm
http://imt.net/~notess/search/index.html
http://www.monash.com/spidap.html

http://www.hamline.edu/library/bush/handouts/
    comparisons.html
http://www.philb.com
http://www.search-secrets.com/
http://techweb.cmp.com/internetwk/
http://newtoo.manifest.com/page1.html
http://biz.yahoo.com/news/internet.html
http://www.cs.rochester.edu/u/ferguson/
    announce.www/
http://netscape.yahoo.com/guide/whats_new.html
http://wwwscout.cs.wisc.edu/scout/report
http://www.whatsnew.com/whatsnew/
http://www.amazon.com
http://bookshop.blackwell.co.uk
http://www.bookshop.co.uk
http://www.tucows.com
http://operasoftware.com
http://www.spycatcher.com
http://www.abc.se/~m9761/bm_conv
http://www.moonsoftware.ee
http://www.goahead.com/gotit/index.htm
http://www.ffg.com/whacker/
http://www.evolve.co.uk/unmozify
http://www.real.com
http://www.adobe.com
http://quicktime.apple.com/
http://www.symantec.co.uk/region/uk/product/
    navbrochure/
http://www.drsolomon.com
http://www.mcafee.com/
http://www.eliashim.com
http://www.ala.org
http://www.aslib.co.uk
http://www.cla.amlibs.ca
http://www.ifla.org
http://www.la-hq.org.uk
http://www.tfpl.com
http://www.yahoo.com/Computers_and_Internet/
    Internet/Magazines

Appendices

Appendix 1 HTML for a search engines home page

In Chapter 11, tip number 29 was to create a new home page providing links to different search engines.

The following HTML code can be used to create such a page for you. Copy it exactly as it has been given, using a simple text editor or a Web authoring tool, and then save it to your local hard disk, giving it a name of your choice, followed by htm as the extension, such as start.htm. Then configure your browser as described in the tip, and you will have a new and hopefully more useful home page!

```
<HTML><HEAD><TITLE>Search Engines Starter Page.</TITLE></HEAD>
<BODY BGCOLOR="#FFFFFF" VLINK="#0000A0" LINK="0000FF">
<CENTER><H2>Search Engines Starter Page.</H2></CENTER>

<P>The search engines listed below will help you find what you are looking for on the
Internet.</P><HR>
<TABLE BORDER="1"><TR><TD COLSTART="1"><H2>General Search
Engines</H2></TD><TD

COLSTART="2"><H2>Name of the Search Engine</H2></TD></TR><TR><TD
ALIGN="RIGHT" ROWSPAN="4" COLSTART="1"><H3>Free text search
engines</H3></TD>

<TD COLSTART="2"><A HREF="http://www.altavista.digital.com/">Alta
Vista</A></TD></TR><TR>
<TD COLSTART="2"><A
HREF="http://www.hotbot.com/">HotBot</A></TD></TR><TR>
<TD COLSTART="2"><A HREF="http://www.lycos.com/">Lycos</A></TD></TR><TR>
<TD COLSTART="2"><A
HREF="http://www.northernlight.com/">Northernlight</A></TD></TR><TR>
<TD ALIGN="RIGHT" ROWSPAN="3" COLSTART="1"><H3>Index based search
engines</H3></TD>
<TD COLSTART="2"><A
HREF="http://www.excite.com/">Excite</A></TD></TR><TR><TD
COLSTART="2"><A
HREF="http://www.metaplus.com/standard.html">Metaplus</A></TD></TR>
<TR><TD COLSTART="2"><A
```

```
HREF="http://www.yahoo.com/">Yahoo</A></TD></TR><TR><TD

ALIGN="RIGHT" ROWSPAN="2" COLSTART="1"><H3>Multi-search
engines</H3></TD><TD

COLSTART="2"><A HREF="http://www.isleuth.com/">Internet
Sleuth</A></TD></TR><TR><TD

COLSTART="2"><A HREF="http://www.inference.com/find">Inference
find</A></TD></TR><TR

><TD ROWSPAN="4" COLSTART="1"><H2>Yellow and White pages</H2></TD><TD

COLSTART="2"><A
HREF="http://www.biography.com/find/find.html">Biographies</A></TD></TR>
<TR><TD COLSTART="2"><A HREF="http://www.eyp.co.uk/">Electronic Yellow
Pages</A></TD></TR>
<TR><TD COLSTART="2"><A
HREF="http://www.Four11.com/">FOUR11</A></TD></TR><TR><TD

COLSTART="2"><A HREF="http://www.whoswho-online.com/search.html">Who's Who
Online</A></TD></TR><TR><TD ROWSPAN="3" COLSTART="1"><H2>Searching for
political/country information</H2></TD><TD COLSTART="2"><A

HREF="http://www.research.att.com/cgi-wald/dbaccess/411">CIA World
Factbook</A></TD></TR>
<TR><TD COLSTART="2"><A
HREF="http://www.muscat.co.uk/">EuroFerret</A></TD></TR><TR

><TD COLSTART="2"><A HREF="http://www.tue.nl/europe/">European
Maps</A></TD></TR><TR

><TD ROWSPAN="7" COLSTART="1"><H2>UK specific resources</H2></TD><TD

COLSTART="2"><A HREF="http://www.open.gov.uk/">British
Government</A></TD></TR><TR

><TD COLSTART="2"><A HREF="http://www.excite.co.uk/">Excite
UK</A></TD></TR><TR><TD

COLSTART="2"><A HREF="http://www.emap.com/id/uk/">Internet Directory
UK</A></TD></TR>
<TR><TD COLSTART="2"><A
HREF="http://www.cybersearch.co.uk/">UKCybersearch</A></TD></TR>
<TR><TD COLSTART="2"><A HREF="http://www.ukindex.co.uk/uksearch.html">UK
Index</A></TD></TR><TR><TD COLSTART="2"><A
HREF="http://uksearch.com/">UKSearch</A></TD></TR>
<TR><TD COLSTART="2"><A HREF="http://www.yahoo.co.uk/">Yahoo
UK</A></TD></TR><TR>
<TD ROWSPAN="3" COLSTART="1"><H2>Searching newsgroups/mail
lists</H2></TD><TD

COLSTART="2"><A HREF="http://www.dejanews.com/">Deja
News</A></TD></TR><TR><TD

COLSTART="2"><A HREF="http://www.liszt.com/">Liszt</A></TD></TR><TR><TD
```

```
COLSTART="2"><A
HREF="http://www.mailbase.ac.uk/">Mailbase</A></TD></TR><TR><TD

ROWSPAN="8" COLSTART="1"><H2>Searching specific resources</H2></TD><TD

COLSTART="2"><A HREF="http://www.ucc.ie/cgi-
bin/acronym">Acronyms</A></TD></TR><TR
><TD COLSTART="2"><A HREF="http://www.gospelcom.net/bible">The
Bible</A></TD></TR>
<TR><TD COLSTART="2"><A
HREF="http://c.gp.cs.cmu.edu:5103/prog/webster">Dictionary
(Websters)</A></TD></TR><TR><TD COLSTART="2"><A

HREF="http://www.edoc.com/ejournal/">Electronic Journals</A></TD></TR><TD

COLSTART="2"><A HREF="http://www.mediauk.com/directory/search.html">MediaUK
(Newspapers/magazines)</A></TD></TR><TR><TD COLSTART="2"><A

HREF="http://lcweb.loc.gov/harvest/">Library of Congress</A></TD></TR><TR><TD

COLSTART="2"><A
HREF="http://www.columbia.edu/acis/bartleby/bartlett/">Quotations</A></TD></TR>
<TR><TD COLSTART="2"><A HREF="http://www.ipl.org/ref/Search.html">Ready
reference collection</A></TD></TR><TR><TD ROWSPAN="2"
COLSTART="1"><H2>Searching
for images/music</H2></TD><TD COLSTART="2"><A
HREF="http://www.lyrics.ch/">Lyrics</A></TD></TR>
<TR><TD COLSTART="2"><A
HREF="http://www.cs.indiana.edu/picons/search.html">Picons
(icons/images)</A></TD></TR><TR><TD ROWSPAN="3"
COLSTART="1"><H2>Searching
for software</H2></TD><TD COLSTART="2"><A
HREF="http://www.shareware.com/">Shareware.com</A></TD></TR>
<TR><TD COLSTART="2"><A
HREF="http://www.filez.com/">Filez.com</A></TD></TR><TR><TD

COLSTART="2"><A
HREF="http://www.download.com/">Download.com</A></TD></TR></TABLE>
<HR></BODY></HTML>
```

Appendix 2   Country codes

AD	Andorra
AE	United Arab Emirates
AF	Afghanistan
AG	Antigua and Barbuda
AI	Anguilla
AL	Albania
AM	Armenia
AN	Netherlands Antilles
AO	Angola
AQ	Antarctica
AR	Argentina
AS	American Samoa
AT	Austria
AU	Australia
AW	Aruba
AZ	Azerbaijan

BA	Bosnia and Herzegovina
BB	Barbados
BD	Bangladesh
BE	Belgium
BF	Burkina Faso
BG	Bulgaria
BH	Bahrain
BI	Burundi
BJ	Benin
BM	Bermuda
BN	Brunei
BO	Bolivia
BR	Brazil
BS	Bahamas
BT	Bhutan

BV	Bouvet Island
BW	Botswana
BY	Belarus
BZ	Belize
CA	Canada
CC	Cocos (Keeling) Islands
CF	Central African Republic
CG	Congo
CH	Switzerland
CI	Côte D'Ivoire (Ivory Coast)
CK	Cook Islands
CL	Chile
CM	Cameroon
CN	China
CO	Colombia
CR	Costa Rica
CS	Czechoslovakia (former)
CU	Cuba
CV	Cape Verde
CX	Christmas Island
CY	Cyprus
CZ	Czech Republic
DE	Germany
DJ	Djibouti
DK	Denmark
DM	Dominica
DO	Dominican Republic
DZ	Algeria
EC	Ecuador
EE	Estonia
EG	Egypt
EH	Western Sahara
ER	Eritrea
ES	Spain
ET	Ethiopia
FI	Finland
FJ	Fiji

FK   Falkland Islands
FM   Micronesia
FO   Faroe Islands
FR   France
FX   France, Metropolitan

GA   Gabon
GB   Great Britain (UK)
GD   Grenada
GE   Georgia
GF   French Guiana
GH   Ghana
GI   Gibraltar
GL   Greenland
GM   Gambia
GN   Guinea
GP   Guadeloupe
GQ   Equatorial Guinea
GR   Greece
GS   South Georgia and South Sandwich Islands.
GT   Guatemala
GU   Guam
GW   Guinea-Bissau
GY   Guyana

HK   Hong Kong
HM   Heard and McDonald Islands
HN   Honduras
HR   Croatia
HT   Haiti
HU   Hungary

ID   Indonesia
IE   Ireland
IL   Israel
IN   India
IO   British Indian Ocean Territory
IQ   Iraq
IR   Iran
IS   Iceland

IT	Italy
JM	Jamaica
JO	Jordan
JP	Japan
KE	Kenya
KG	Kyrgyzstan
KH	Cambodia
KI	Kiribati
KM	Comoros
KN	Saint Kitts and Nevis
KP	Korea (North)
KR	Korea (South)
KW	Kuwait
KY	Cayman Islands
KZ	Kazakhstan
LA	Laos
LB	Lebanon
LC	Saint Lucia
LI	Liechtenstein
LK	Sri Lanka
LR	Liberia
LS	Lesotho
LT	Lithuania
LU	Luxembourg
LV	Latvia
LY	Libya
MA	Morocco
MC	Monaco
MD	Moldova
MG	Madagascar
MH	Marshall Islands
MK	Macedonia
ML	Mali
MM	Myanmar (Burma)
MN	Mongolia
MO	Macau

MP	Northern Mariana Islands
MQ	Martinique
MR	Mauritania
MS	Montserrat
MT	Malta
MU	Mauritius
MV	Maldives
MW	Malawi
MX	Mexico
MY	Malaysia
MZ	Mozambique
NA	Namibia
NATO	Nato field
NC	New Caledonia
NE	Niger
NF	Norfolk Island
NG	Nigeria
NI	Nicaragua
NL	Netherlands
NO	Norway
NP	Nepal
NR	Nauru
NT	Neutral Zone
NU	Niue
NZ	New Zealand
OM	Oman
PA	Panama
PE	Peru
PF	French Polynesia
PG	Papua New Guinea
PH	Philippines
PK	Pakistan
PL	Poland
PM	St Pierre and Miquelon
PN	Pitcairn
PR	Puerto Rico
PT	Portugal

PW	Palau
PY	Paraguay
QA	Qatar
RE	Réunion
RO	Romania
RU	Russian Federation
RW	Rwanda
SA	Saudi Arabia
SB	Solomon Islands
SC	Seychelles
SD	Sudan
SE	Sweden
SG	Singapore
SH	St Helena
SI	Slovenia
SJ	Svalbard and Jan Mayen Islands
SK	Slovak Republic
SL	Sierra Leone
SM	San Marino
SN	Senegal
SO	Somalia
SR	Suriname
ST	Saõ Tomé and Príncipe
SU	USSR (former)
SV	El Salvador
SY	Syria
SZ	Swaziland
TC	Turks and Caicos Islands
TD	Chad
TF	French Southern Territories
TG	Togo
TH	Thailand
TJ	Tajikistan
TK	Tokelau
TM	Turkmenistan
TN	Tunisia

TO	Tonga
TP	East Timor
TR	Turkey
TT	Trinidad and Tobago
TV	Tuvalu
TW	Taiwan
TZ	Tanzania
UA	Ukraine
UG	Uganda
UK	United Kingdom
UM	US Minor Outlying Islands
US	United States
UY	Uruguay
UZ	Uzbekistan
VA	Vatican City State
VC	Saint Vincent and the Grenadines
VE	Venezuela
VG	Virgin Islands (British)
VI	Virgin Islands (US)
VN	Vietnam
VU	Vanuatu
WF	Wallis and Futuna Islands
WS	Samoa
YE	Yemen
YT	Mayotte
YU	Yugoslavia
ZA	South Africa
ZM	Zambia
ZR	Democratic Republic of Congo (formerly Zaïre)
ZW	Zimbabwe

Appendix 3 URLs mentioned in the book

Chapter 1 An introduction to the Internet

http://www.yahoo.com/Computers_and_Internet/
    Internet/History/
http://www.anamorph.com/docs/stats/stats.html
http://www.matisse.net/files/glossary.html
http://www.w3c.org/

Chapter 2 An introduction to search engines

http://www.quoteland.com/index.html
http://www.isleuth.com
http://www.metaplus.com
http://www.altavista.digital.com
http://www.yahoo.com
http://www.metaplus.com
http://www.searchenginewatch.com
http://www.amazon.com

Chapter 3 Free text search engines

http://www.altavista.digital.com.
http://www.lycos.com
http://www.hotbot.com
http://www.euroferret.com
http://www.aol.com/netfind/
http://www.search.com
http://www.excite.com/
http://www.goto.com

http://www.euroseek.com
http://www.infoseek.com
http://www.looksmart.com
http://www.northernlight.com
http://www.searcheurope.com
http://www.surfstorm.com
http://www.webcrawler.com

Chapter 4 Index-based search engines

http://www.yahoo.com
http://www.yahoo.co.uk
http://www.mckinley.com
http://www.net-find.com
http://www.god.co.uk
http://www.snap.com.
http://galaxy.tradewave.com
http://www.nosearch.com

Chapter 5 Multi-search engines and more!

http://www.metaplus.com
http://www.isleuth.com
http://www.infind.com/
http://www.metaspy.com
http://bible.gospelcom.net/
http://work.ucsd.edu:5141/cgi-bin/http_webster
http://www.ipl.org/ref/Search.html
http://www.four11.com
http://www.bigfoot.com

Chapter 6 Other available database resources

http://www.silverplatter.com
http://www.forrester.com
http://www.ovid.com
http://www.chadwyck.co.uk
http://www.biomednet.com
http://chemweb.com

http://www.ariadne.ac.uk
http://www.hw.ac.uk/libWWW/irn/irn.html
http://www.slate.com
http://www.economist.com
http://www.ft.com
http://www.telegraph.co.uk
http://www.amazon.com
http://www.northernlight.com/
http://www.hammond.co.uk
http://www.btarray.bt.com
http://www.internet-magazine.com/buy/
http://www.pulver.com/million/

Chapter 7 Virtual libraries and gateways

http://www.philb.com
http://vlib.stanford.edu/Overview.html
http://www.w3.org/vl/
http://www.mth.uea.ac.uk/VL/Overview.html
http://www.ukoln.ac.uk/services/elib/
http://www.jisc.ac.uk
http://www.ilrt.bris.ac.uk/roads/who/
http://www.adam.ac.uk
http://sunsite.berkeley.edu/~emorgan/alex
http://www.bized.ac.uk
http://www.ilrt.bris.ac.uk/crn/
http://www.ub2.lu.se/eel/eelhome.html
http://www.eevl.ac.uk
http://www.uku.fi/kirjasto/virtuaalikirjasto/
http://ihr.sas.ac.uk
http://www.netskills.ac.uk/NETEG/
http://www.omni.ac.uk
http://osl.os.qub.ac.uk
http://rudi.herts.ac.uk
http://www.sosig.ac.uk/
http://www.cleanh2o.com/cleanh2o/ww/
    welcome.html
http://users.ox.ac.uk/~humbul
http://www.scran.ac.uk/cgi-bin/links/view.pl
http://www.bubl.ac.uk

Chapter 8 Intelligent agents

http://www.chatter-bots.com
http://www.firefly.net/
http://www.filmfinder.com/
http://www.shoppingexplore.com
http://www.crayon.net
http://www.agentware.com
http://www.yahoo.com
http://www.excite.com
http://www.personal.lycos.com
http://www.wired.com/newbot/personal_agent.html
http://www.qdeck.com
http://www.alexa.com

Chapter 9 Usenet newsgroups and mailing lists

http://www.yahoo.com/Computers_and_Internet/
    Software/Internet/Usenet
http://www.forteinc.com
http://www.dejanews.com
http://www.liszt.com
http://www.neosoft.com/internet/paml/default.html
ftp://rtfm.mit.edu/pub/usenet-by-group/
    news.lists.misc/
http://www.mailbase.ac.uk
http://www.jisc.ac.uk

Chapter 10 The information mix and into the future

http://www.dyslexiaonline.com/center.html
http://www.imdb.com
http://www.metaplus.com
http://www.dailywav.com/
http://sound-ring.com/index.html
http://www.mailbase.ac.uk
http://www.open.gov.uk
http://www.timeout.co.uk.
http://www.telegraph.co.uk

http://www.dataware.com

Chapter 11 Thirty tips and hints for better and quicker searching

http://www.netmind.com/URL-minder/
  URL-minder.html
http://www.philb.com/

Chapter 12 Sources for further help and assistance

http://www.searchenginewatch.com
http://webreference.com/
http://events.internet.com
http://www.conferences.calendar.com
http://www.browserwatch.internet.com
http://www.InternetNews.com/
http://www.cnet.com
http://www.zdnet.com
http://www.zdu.com
http://www.december.com/cmc/info/
http://thelist.internet.com/
http://www.thedirectory.org/
http://ciac.llnl.gov/ciac/CIACHoaxes.html
http://www.fau.edu/rinaldi/netiquette.html
http://www.matisse.net/files/glossary.html
http://www.mailbase.ac.uk
http://www.liszt.com
http://www.junkemail.org/scamspam/
http://www.ftc.gov
http://oasis.ot.com/~dmuth/spam-l
http://spam.abuse.net/
http://www4.zdnet.com/anchordesk/story/
  story_index_19970819.html
http://www.csn.net/~felbel/jnkmail.html
http://www.dis.strath.ac.uk/business/search.html
http://www.unn.ac.uk/features.htm
http://imt.net/~notess/search/index.html
http://www.monash.com/spidap.html

http://www.hamline.edu/library/bush/handouts/
    comparisons.html
http://www.philb.com
http://www.search-secrets.com/
http://www.internetnews.com
http://techweb.cmp.com/internetwk/
http://newtoo.manifest.com/page1.html
http://biz.yahoo.com/news/internet.html
http://www.cs.rochester.edu/u/ferguson/
    announce.www/
http://netscape.yahoo.com/guide/whats_new.html
http://wwwscout.cs.wisc.edu/scout/report
http://www.whatsnew.com/whatsnew/
http://www.amazon.com
http://bookshop.blackwell.co.uk
http://www.bookshop.co.uk
http://www.tucows.com
http://operasoftware.com
http://www.spycatcher.com
http://www.abc.se/~m9761/bm_conv
http://www.moonsoftware.ee
http://www.goahead.com/gotit/index.htm
http://www.ffg.com/whacker/
http://www.evolve.co.uk/unmozify
http://www.real.com
http://www.adobe.com
http://quicktime.apple.com/
http://www/symantec.co.uk/region/uk/product/
    newbrochure
http://www.drsolomon.com
http://www.mcafee.com/
http://www.eliashim.com
http://www.ala.org
http://www.aslib.co.uk
http://www.cla.amlibs.ca
http://www.ifla.org
http://www.la-hq.org.uk
http://www.tfpl.com

Index